Mourning Break

Mourning Break

Words of Hope for Those in Grief

Rev. Betsy Haas and Lisa Mahaffey

WestBow
PRESS
A DIVISION OF THOMAS NELSON

ISBN: 9781449760489 (hc)
ISBN: 9781449760496 (sc)
ISBN: 9781449760502 (e)

Library of Congress Control Number: 2012914285

WestBow Press books may be ordered through booksellers or by contacting:

WestBow Press
A Division of Thomas Nelson
1663 Liberty Drive
Bloomington, IN 47403
www.westbowpress.com
1-(866) 928-1240

Because of the dynamic nature of the Internet, any web addresses or links contained in
this book may have changed since publication and may no longer be valid. The views
expressed in this work are solely those of the author and do not necessarily reflect the views
of the publisher, and the publisher hereby disclaims any responsibility for them.

Any people depicted in stock imagery provided by Thinkstock are models,
and such images are being used for illustrative purposes only.

Certain stock imagery © Thinkstock.

Scripture references are from the following sources:

The Holy Bible, New International Version ® (NIV). Copyright © 1973, 1978, 1984 by
International Bible Society. Used by permission of Zondervan. All rights reserved. King James
Version (KJV), copyright © 1979, 1980, 1982, Thomas Nelson Publishers. The Message (MSG)
by Eugene H. Peterson, copyright © 1993, 1994, 1995, 1996, 2000. Used by permission of
NavPress Publishing Group. The Amplified Bible: Old Testament (AMP), copyright © 1962,
1964, 1965, 1987 by the Zondervan Corporation (used by permission); and The Amplified
New Testament, copyright © 1958 by the Lockman Foundation (used by permission). New
American Standard Bible ® (NASB), copyright © 1960, 1962, 1963, 1968, 1971, 1973, 1975,
1977, 1995 by The Lockman Foundation. New Century Version ® (NCV), copyright 1987,
1988, 1991, 2005 by Thomas Nelson, Inc. Used by permission. All rights reserved. The Holy
Bible, New Living Translation (NLT), copyright © 1996. Used by permission of Tyndale
House Publishers, Inc., Wheaton, Illinois 60189. All rights reserved. The Contemporary English
Version (CEV), copyright © 1991 by the American Bible Society. Used by permission.

Printed in the United States of America

WestBow Press rev. date: 10/01/2012

Acknowledgments

From Lisa and Betsy:

To our Lord and Savior, Jesus Christ, with praise and thanksgiving for Who you are in our lives. Thank you for what You have done through the pain and sorrow of the grief of many, for the comfort of all. This is for Your glory.

John, Becky, Kelly, Sherry, Tom, Michael, and Ann – thank you for opening up your hearts and sharing your personal stories of grief and loss through long hours of interviews. You will be a blessing to others with this gift of encouragement as they hear your stories.

Jeannie Cooper – our super editor. You rock! We can't thank you enough for the countless hours of editing and for sharing your gifts with us, and for believing in us first.

Sabrina – our graphic design artist. Thank you for blessing us with our beautiful cover design. We are grateful for your help with this project and for waking up at dawn to capture the most amazing sunrise photo.

From Lisa:

Rev. Betsy Haas – my friend, pastor, and mentor. Thank you for believing in me and giving me the most amazing opportunity to lead Grief Share. If it weren't for that ministry, I would not have collected these amazing stories. You have been my rock and my cheerleader – someone I look up to for wisdom and guidance. Thank you for your incredible insight into the emergent themes of these chapters, but most of all thank you for putting up with my impatience while getting this project finished.

Mike – my husband and best friend. You encouraged me to pursue my dream and even bought me a video camera to record interviews with. Thank you for always taking the time to listen to me ramble and for being my sounding board.

From Betsy:

My husband, Kenn, the love of my life and my quiet and steadfast supporter; and my daughters Sarah and Jamie; for sharing their Mom with others, sometimes at their own expense.

Lisa, the brain-child of this book. Thank you for your vision and your singular belief in the promise of this book. Your tireless efforts to get it completed are the only reason this happened. Thank you for your confidence in my writing ability and especially for your unconditional friendship.

Contents

Introduction
Lisa Mahaffey

It was Wednesday night and the season finale of the 1990s television drama *Melrose Place* was about to begin. I sighed as I paced back and forth and stared out the dining room window. My husband Matt was late as usual getting home from work. Didn't he know I was counting on him to watch our baby so I could meet up with girlfriends in time for the show to begin? As a new mom I rarely had the opportunity for a night out with the girls and this was a special one.

The phone rang and instead of his usual apology for being late I was greeted by a different and very stressed voice telling me something had happened to Matt at work. What could have happened? Matt worked in his family's auto repair business. He often spoke of shady characters that would lurk around at dusk admiring the customer's exotic, foreign cars he was securing for the night. Could someone have robbed him? Stabbed him? Run over him? I rushed next door to see if my dependable neighbor Mel would mind watching the baby while I went to see what happened. My mind worked up into such a frenzy I could hardly stop my leg from shaking uncontrollably as I tried to push the accelerator pedal down on my green Mercury Villager minivan.

I pulled out my cell phone to call my friend Jan, who was hosting the girl's night out. I needed her to know I wouldn't be at the party, but most of all I needed someone to talk to—someone to calm me down as my mind imagined the worst of scenarios. As I arrived at the shop there were rescue vehicles blocking the street and blinding my eyes with tons of flashing red and blue lights. Firefighters rushed to my car door as I anxiously stepped out of the car. They informed me that Matt was inside the building, but despite my desperate pleas they would not allow me in. "We're working on him," the paramedic informed me. My first glimpse of Matt came as rescue workers threw open the door and rolled out the stretcher with his blue, lifeless body on it. An odd- looking machine was resting on his chest performing automatic cardiac compressions.

The fire chief gently approached me with the news, "It appears your husband went into cardiac arrest. You can follow us to the hospital." Thankfully my friend Jan had taken the initiative to leave her party and come to the auto shop. She drove me to the hospital as we followed the ambulance. Upon arriving there I was prevented from joining my husband back in the ER. Distraught, I looked up from my hard plastic seat in the waiting room to find my dad walking through the automatic door. He had driven by the shop as he usually did on his way home from work to say hello to Matt and learned of the news. At the age of 26, I was not prepared to hear, "I'm sorry, we've done all we can" from the emergency room nurse. After all, my life was just beginning; our life was just beginning with our one-year-old son, Brett.

My dad and I were finally led back in the emergency room to see Matt lying on a table lifeless and blue. He was gone – already home with his Lord and Savior. I've never seen my dad cry before, but in that moment it was all we could do. After the funeral and initial shock, I remember thinking, "What am I going to do? How am I going to get through this? Why am I struggling if I have faith? How will I pay bills with two mortgages and no life insurance?"

Fellow church members, co-workers, and family all tried to reach out and help but unless you've been there it's hard to truly understand.

How many other twenty-six-year-old widows would I find to talk to who could relate? None, I thought.

Fearing that my pain of grief would equate to weak faith, I hid those emotions from the outside world and put on a false front for everyone to see. The only help I reached out for in the beginning was a private counselor but I found little comfort there. I leaned on a couple of close friends whose greatest gift to me was just listening—listening when I needed to ramble and repeat myself over and over, trying to accept the finality that I was in fact a widow. Night after night I got on my knees and prayed to God for strength and for clarity about what had just happened. I blurted out that often-asked "why" question – Why me? Why now? Why did You do this? In my pain, I was blaming God for allowing Matt to die, because I knew He had the power to heal if He wanted to. Lost in my pain and self-pity, I missed the benefits of the relationship God wanted with me.

The months following Matt's death would be a pivotal time in my life. I held tightly to God's word, and prayed so often that I felt like God was the only person I spoke to all day. Slowly I began to feel the amazing presence of the Holy Spirit at work in my life. When I felt as though there was nowhere else to turn, I turned toward God and leaned in hard, finding the loving, open arms of my Abba Father. He taught me so much about myself and about His desire for my life—a life that didn't consist of me drowning in a sea of self-pity.

With the grace of God, I learned to take baby steps toward understanding that what I used to have was merely a religion, but now I had tapped into the most life-transforming gift – an intimate, love-filled relationship with my Lord and Savior, Jesus Christ. This relationship filled my sails with a strong, fresh wind that propelled me to go on living. Through the gift of grief God drew me so close to Him and gave me a faith like never before. I saw God's hand at work in my life, and there was no mistaking who was in control–and it was good!

God brought amazing blessings into my life in His perfect timing. I moved from the "Why me?" prayers to the "Whatever Lord" prayers, and I asked Him to do with my life whatever He wanted. That is when my life began to change. I submitted to God's plan and gave up the desire to be in control of my destiny. It was scary but exciting at the same time. God taught me how to be happy being me—single me—if that was His plan. It was a great place to be. Joy had finally returned!

Yet God's plans for my life would bring new blessings, when three years later He orchestrated a chance encounter with a wonderful Christian man who later became my husband and father of Brett along with two additional children. We were a happy family of five. Life was good, but I felt God whispering to me and telling me to stretch beyond my life as a wife, mother, and volunteer. I began to wrestle with my purpose here on Earth. How was God going to use me? The Bible says in Romans 8:28, "And we know that in all things God works for the good of those who love Him, who have been called according to His purpose." (NIV 1984) I reminded myself of the "all things" and pondered about how God could use my loss for something good.

As time passed, whenever I heard of someone losing a loved one my heart would sink into a place of compassion. I could almost feel the heaviness of grief as if it were happening to me all over again. I found myself wanting to write letters even to strangers to offer some small measure of comfort and encouragement because I knew what it felt like to be in that place. If I could share my story maybe it would offer hope to others to see that with God anything is possible, and through

His love and comfort it is possible to go on living when someone you love dies.

When I began writing, words just flowed out of me like never before. Ask any of my grade school teachers and they would tell you that writing was not one of my strong points. I came to understand God was answering my prayer of "whatever Lord," using me as His vehicle to bring comfort to grieving hearts. Knowing that I could make a difference in someone else's life brought sunshine into my day. This new ministry was a step in the direction of God's purpose for my life, but I felt called to do more.

It wasn't long after my new husband and I moved from Florida to Georgia in 2002 that I enrolled my children in the local public school. I introduced myself to the school guidance counselor. Through getting to know each other, I shared my story of loss with her. One thing led to another and I was approached with the idea of facilitating a weekly support group for children dealing with grief. The school would even pay the costs for the facilitator training. Could I do it? Could I help kids learn how to deal with the emotions of grief? What a great opportunity to expand God's purpose for my life to use my grief for something good.

Children came together through this program and shared their feelings in a safe place, often expressing thoughts and emotions they were uncomfortable discussing with family. I witnessed the therapeutic benefits of bringing kids together with like-experiences and how that validated their feelings. They realized they were not alone and greatly benefited from learning that others in their own school struggled with some of the same issues they were facing. As I invested my time helping these sweet children I was the one who was being blessed. Famous Christian author Barbara Johnson coined the phrase "boomerang blessings," which simply means when you bless others it will come back to you. I was living the boomerang blessing philosophy and I found myself thanking God for leading me to this ministry opportunity. I was learning about God's timing, which is always perfect.

Through my work with the children at the school, I often wondered about the families they belonged to and how they were coping with their grief. If bringing children together with like experiences helped, what about doing the same for adults? Shortly after pondering that question, God pointed me in a direction where I would find His perfect answer.

Because we were new to the town, my family visited local churches in search of a place to call home. As we joined a local United Methodist Church, the membership process included a meeting with the Associate Pastor, Rev. Betsy Haas. During our meeting I expressed my desire to get involved in the church and specifically I wanted to know if they had any grief-type programs where I could volunteer. I'm not sure who was more excited, Betsy or me, but apparently the church owned materials for a well-known grief support program but had never put the course into place. Another person had also come forward expressing interest so the two of us joined forces to launch a weekly support group for adults. The six years that I was involved with this grief program turned out to be the greatest blessing in my life. God gave me the amazing privilege to be a facilitator of His word to others and to watch the Body of Christ at work uplifting and encouraging each other like cheerleaders on a Friday night football field. At the end of every 14-week class there was always this part of me that was saddened as I sent those I had shepherded back into the world to finish the journey called grief.

God had done such amazing things in my life through my loss that I knew He would do the same for others. Another famous quote from author Barbara Johnson says, "We grow when we're down in the valley because that's where the fertilizer is." God uses even times of pain and sadness to draw us near to Him, and when we exercise our faith in the darkness it's a priceless gift to God. It is in those valleys where we are able to grow.

One of the joys of facilitating the support group was receiving correspondence from past participants. They would write to share encouraging news of how their lives were changing in a positive way. This was the exact hope for better days I had tried to impart to them throughout the course, but many who were weighted down by grief could not grasp the idea until later. These stories were so precious to me that I saved them all in an organized vinyl three-ring binder. Whenever I'd have a bad day, I would just pull out that binder and I would instantly be encouraged by the amazing testimonies. They were too good not to be shared so God nudged me to stop collecting them for myself and to start sharing them.

I arranged for past participants from the grief group to attend the first night of a new class. My intent was for the past participants to encourage the new ones with real-life personal testimony. I was thinking small, but God was thinking BIG. Those testimonies had such an impact on the new group that I began to see how more grievers could be encouraged by collecting the stories on paper. I began to think, What if I put all these stories together into a book and could get a copy into the hands of every grieving person? With God nothing is impossible, thus began the process of writing this book. As I shared this excitement with my mentor and pastor Rev. Haas, she came up with an even better idea—we'd collaborate together where I'd collect and write the stories, and she would tie in God's word to each story, giving grievers a reference point in the Bible to turn to. It would be the first book of its kind.

Although the names and places have been modified for privacy reasons, the stories contained in this book are real-life accounts of people I personally know, who found through grief that our God is an awesome God who can AND does use all things for the good of those who love Him. My prayer is that through these stories you will be encouraged to see that losing a loved one is not the end but rather a new beginning. God's purpose for your life after loss will go far beyond what you could ever imagine if you trust Him and allow Him to show you the way.

Introduction continued….
Rev. Betsy Haas

I still remember that moment when in the midst of a "new church member" meeting Lisa mentioned her desire to volunteer in my church's grief ministry….a ministry that was greatly needed, but didn't yet exist. Lisa was like a lovely piece of manna dropped down from heaven to bring sustenance and hope to people wandering in the desert of mourning. We began offering a grief recovery class that next fall, and literally hundreds of people found wholeness over the next six years. From that experience Mourning Break was born and you have before you seven of their stories as told to Lisa. Following each testimony is a chapter that I wrote which follows the emergent theological theme that was evident in each person's experience.

My own life took a significant turn during the writing of this book. In the space of three years my oldest child was diagnosed with cancer and had to undergo months of debilitating chemotherapy. A few months later our dog of thirteen years died. Then my position at the church where I had served for sixteen years was eliminated during a staff restructuring. In haste my husband and I decided to move to a place far away, which we did only two months after leaving my church. Two months later my oldest, now recovered from her cancer, got married and moved several states away. Then two months after the wedding my world truly exploded when my father died.

I found myself in that beautifully awful place where I had nothing familiar around me. There was nothing normal to structure my day and very little that looked or felt "right." I was in a wilderness place experiencing a drought of joy and an absence of peace. I was grieving and suddenly I realized that I was not just writing about mourning, but living it. And it was here that I learned that when everything that means "life" to you is suddenly removed, there is God. God became more present to me in the absence of everything else then at any other time in my life.

The chapters I have written here are straight from God Himself. I look back at some of the early words that were written in the beginning of this journey and I don't even recognize them, just as a scribe would not recognize a scroll that had been dictated by the Master years earlier. They are His words, not mine.

It is my fervent prayer that through these words, you find healing for your hurt, hope for your future, and the promise of peace that Christ died to ensure you would have…just as they did for me.

If you have a story to share or comment about the book, please go to our website, www.mourningbreak.com or Facebook page "Mourning Break," and post a comment.

CHAPTER ONE

John

Nobody is immune to grief—not even pastors. Grief is a part of life—it is the cost of loving someone. Have you ever thought about what it must be like for pastors to lose someone they love? Is it any easier for them? They are usually the ones who console others during a loss, officiate at funerals, make those late-night hospital visits when someone is sick, and who are there to listen to grieving church members pour out their hurting hearts. But to whom do pastors turn when they suffer a tragic loss?

Often people perceive grief as a sign of weakness and Christians mistakenly reason if they have a strong faith then they shouldn't be grieving. On the contrary Jesus wept at the tomb of a dear friend and set the example for us all to follow.

So what is a pastor to do in times of immense personal grief? What would happen if a pastor got angry with God for taking a loved one to Heaven? What would church members think if they found out?

This story is a love story cut short by cancer, a story of immense grief and anger, a story of purpose in God's plan not to waste our suffering, and a story that evolved into a seminary thesis and subsequent book made possible only through the personal experience of having walked through a journey of grief.

John Whitton, youth pastor at Westwood Christian Church, embarked on a church mission trip in 1994—a trip where he would find the love of his life. "I had waited a long time to get married. I was an old bachelor," says John. But John discovered on the mission trip that he had found that special person, and on March 30, 1996, John Whitton and Leah Smith exchanged vows. John had concerns about being 12 years older than Leah. "We talked about that an awful lot—the implications of that," says John, but they didn't let it stop them from planning to serve in ministry, begin a family, and grow old with each other for the rest of their lives.

John and Leah began serving side by side in a multitude of ministries. As newlyweds, they planned out the perfect life—when they would buy a house, how soon they would start a family, etc. Everything was falling into place—or so it seemed. However, in November of 1997—about a year and a half into their marriage—Leah began to experience vision problems. Tests revealed that Leah had an inoperable malignant brain tumor. "I'll never forget the day when the surgeon met us in the conference room, gave us the word on the biopsy, and then basically said it's bad. He gave her less than a year to live," says John. The news was devastating considering Leah was only twenty-eight years old and a picture of absolute health.

John and Leah knew what they had to do—they embarked on a journey to save Leah's life. John poured over medical research and spent countless hours reading anything and everything he could about this type of cancer. In the midst of dealing with chemo and radiation, Leah also had to cope with paralyzing stroke-like symptoms on her left side caused by a biopsy bleed. It would take six to eight months before she would regain most of her motor functions. Contrary to medical predictions, Leah favorably responded to the treatments. The tumor shrank by 90%, putting her into a four-year remission – something unheard of with her diagnosis.

During that four-year remission, Leah would return to the doctor every three months for a scan, because the doctors were certain the cancer would return. John says, "And so we lived with that—we lived life in three-month increments. For about eleven weeks we'd be good, but the week before the scan we'd get nervous. When we received a good report (a good scan) we'd celebrate, relax, and breathe." However in January 2002 the cancer returned just as the doctor had predicted. From 2002 through 2005, Leah underwent continuous chemotherapy. Determined to overcome the disease, John and Leah gathered up all her scans and traveled throughout the country, meeting with numerous physicians. Everywhere they traveled, doctors would comment at how miraculous it was for Leah to be alive.

"The last year of Leah's life she began to decline," said John. "Her body couldn't take it anymore. She had so much chemo and radiation." Leah went from walking with a cane, to a walker, to a wheelchair, and finally to a hospital bed set up through hospice in their home. On May 11, 2005, Leah passed away, seven and a half years after the initial diagnosis that predicted she had one year to live. "It was a really tough journey," said John. "I was devastated. I knew it was coming, but I had not accepted it. The whole focus of my existence for all those years was to try to save my wife's life every day."

Grief consumed John to the point that he was not able to sleep, especially in his own home. He couldn't eat, lost a significant amount of weight in just a few months, and although he would not describe himself as a person who cries, he remembers crying all the time after Leah's death. John describes it as an, "intense sobbing, aching hurt in your gut 24/7, not caring whether a bus ran over you type of feeling." And John was not new to grief. While Leah was sick for those seven and a half years, John lost both his sister and his mother to cancer. But because John was so consumed with Leah's care, he wasn't able to properly grieve those other losses. He was not expecting the loss of Leah to be magnified by the unresolved grief over his sister and mother.

"So, when it was all said and done, all three hit me—boom," said John. "The loss that hit me the hardest was my wife. I became very angry. I was so mad. The anger almost consumed me." With thoughts he might not make it through this unfamiliar process, John took a proactive approach way beyond his comfort zone. He grudgingly sought out a Christian grief support group at a church 20 miles away, providing anonymity and safety. Others in the group remember John staring at the floor week after week. John would later recall his thoughts after that first meeting, *The first time I came to the support group I said I'd never come back. The second time I said I'd never come back, but then I became determined—I knew I had to if I was going to survive. As I stuck with it, I found it was the one place I could go where I knew people understood what it was like.* The group could see anger and bitterness in John, but he offered no details of his story. It would take six weeks for John to open himself up to the group and share, including the revelation that he was a pastor.

Others were naturally curious as to why John the pastor, was angry. People generally tend to put pastors on a pedestal where they are viewed as perfect and expected to be free from emotional distress because of their calling. The truth is they are just like anyone else— they are human beings with the same emotions God created in everyone. As John slowly opened up to the group, he revealed more about his anger and how it was directed at God, because Leah was the one to suffer the devastating cancer.

Still struggling intellectually and spiritually, John prematurely returned to his duties at the church. He remembers an encounter with a church member a few months after Leah died. A sweet, older woman gently approached him to inquire how he was. Unfortunately, she was not prepared for John's response to her question as he fired back with, "I wish I were dead." Shortly following that reply, church leadership approached John and gracefully offered him a much-needed sabbatical. John had been a faithful employee for over twenty years and agreed that time apart would be very beneficial.

"The first year was a horrible time—It's tough," said John. First things came along like anniversaries, birthdays, and holidays like Christmas, but John didn't feel like celebrating and instead would travel to local missions to serve food to the homeless. Looking back on it, John said, "It was the most devastating event of my life. I had to get through a ton of stuff—my anger being the most critical thing I had to deal with. I read everything I could get my hands on about grief and suffering." John found some books were helpful and some were not. While he took a proactive approach to trying to find healing including individual counseling, group therapy, and pouring over numerous grief-recovery books, he knew that ultimately he had to come to grips with this anger at God. "I had to say logically that I don't understand this, I don't like it, but if I'm mad at God— well, you can't be mad at God and not believe in Him," said John. "If I was mad at Him and directing anger at Him, I'm acknowledging that He's there. And if He's there, I'm acknowledging that there's something beyond this life. And if there's something beyond, that implies immortality, the eternal, and that He's the source of it. Therefore, I finally had to come to the conclusion that since He was the only hope of my seeing Leah again in eternity, then I couldn't stay mad at Him forever."

John realized his healing would involve deliberate choice on a daily basis to believe and follow God even when he didn't understand and couldn't see God's plans. He likened his situation to Job's character in the Bible who wasn't privy to understanding the tests he would be subjected to. There is an eternal significance in some of our experiences in this earthly life, and we will clearly understand the purpose of these experiences in God's timing. John understood this and embraced it in his desire to keep moving through the journey called grief.

During his sabbatical, John visited and observed other church's worship services to collect research and finally complete his unfinished Master of Divinity thesis. In nine months, he visited fifty churches. This thesis opened doors for John to write and publish his own grief book in 2007. In a desire to pass along the help he gleaned from pouring over numerous grief-recovery books, John compiled pertinent information and summarized each text's main points in a way useful to others. This book would not only carry on Leah's legacy, but it would be a vital resource for fellow grievers as they struggled through the healing process.

Each carefully organized chapter reviewed a particular grief recovery book. John also included an introduction that recounted his own personal story of grief. "A lot of the grief books I read didn't satisfy me. So my motivation in writing what I wrote was to go out there and get my hands on books and review this stuff, picking out the best that's out there," John said.

Using a connection with a publishing house while working on a church-related project, John discovered the publishing process wasn't nearly as complicated as he once thought. In his first print run, John published 330 copies that sold out within five months.

Writing this book became a huge part of John's healing process. He reflected on where he needed to keep his focus, "And that focus is on our faith in Christ, the assurance of his resurrection, the hope we have of seeing our loved ones again because we know they are with Him, and Christ is alive. Our loved ones are in a place where they not only are free of any suffering they had here on this earth, but they are also in a place where they understand it all. We don't understand it, but they do. That's a great comfort." What a wonderful gift John has left for all who walk the same journey of grief. Because of his experience, John's testimony gives a credible offering of proof that healing can and will occur. But John didn't stop at publishing a book.

John arrived at a point on his journey where he desired to pass along the hope to others in a more personal way. He began a grief support program at his home church and began facilitating weekly sessions to help others. John's life experience made him the perfect candidate. He'd also been around his church for twenty-five years as a pastor, and prior to that he was also a member there. Church members began to look at John as a frame of reference. "The congregation would look at me and say here's a guy who we've known and seen all these years, and we also were there when he met and fell in love with his wife," says John. "We saw the magical courtship they had and we saw them serving together, and we saw the devastating diagnosis she got." With that frame of reference, people trusted John's expertise when it came to the subject of mourning, reminiscent of the old commercial: "When E.F. Hutton speaks, people listen." Through losing Leah to cancer, John was able to bring that experience to the table with his own congregation.

God took the tragic event of John losing Leah and used that experience to bring help and hope to others through John's book and through the new program he started at his church. God never wastes our sufferings. He always finds a way, if we are faithful, to reveal to us a place where we can take the pain of our loss and use it for His good, bringing hope and help to His kingdom on earth. We are merely instruments of his sweet grace, and sometimes we can only play the song because we've sat unwillingly in the practice room for days on end and have chosen to be obedient to what God can do through it. John's journey through grief gives new meaning to the old hymn

"Amazing Grace"—*amazing grace, how sweet the sound, that saved a wretch like me, I once was lost, but now am found, was blind but now I see.* John now views life from a new perspective. He is no longer lost in grief, but now sees a whole new opportunity for ministry laid out before him which God Himself orchestrated through the experience of his wife's death.

When asked what Bible verse would summarize his journey, John reflected: "I would have to say it is a passage and not just a verse. The passage is 2 Corinthians 4:7-18. If I had to narrow it down within that passage, I would pick verses 16-18 which says: "Therefore we do not lose heart. Though outwardly we are wasting away, yet inwardly we are being renewed day by day. Our light and momentary troubles are achieving for us an eternal glory that far outweighs them all. So we fix our eyes not on what is seen, but on what is unseen. For what is seen is temporary, but what is unseen is eternal.""

Anger
Rev. Haas

When I was growing up, my mother liked to cook things quickly in a pot known as a pressure cooker. The pressure cooker was a heavy metal pot with an even heavier metal lid that clamped on to seal in the contents. On the top of the lid was a release valve known as a toggle; you stuck a fork in the hole of the toggle and twisted it to the side, releasing the steam that had built up in the pot. Pots needed to be toggled periodically to maintain a safe amount of pressurized steam in the pot, which cooked the ingredients more quickly than conventional methods. In short, pressure cookers were a kind of nineteen-sixty's version of the microwave.

One Saturday morning, my mother was cooking her wonderful vegetable soup in the pressure cooker. Every thirty minutes she would toggle the release valve for a few minutes and then go about other chores. The phone rang and one of my mother's friends was on the other line. She had fallen off a stepladder and needed a ride to the emergency room with an injured ankle, and so my mother headed out to assist her, leaving my father in charge of the pressure cooker.

Unfortunately the Phillies were on TV that day, and Dad got immersed in balls and strikes and forgot to go into the kitchen to toggle the release valve. The resulting explosion of heavy metal lid and ten quarts of cabbage, chopped vegetables and brown broth pretty much coated the entire kitchen, and left a significant dent in the wall where the lid had gone flying. Dad and I spent three hours cleaning soup off the walls, counters, cabinets and floor, and twenty years later when we finally replaced the old wallpaper we found fossilized cabbage pieces embedded in a far corner of the room.

This story is offered as an illustration of the power of anger. Left 'untoggled,' its pressure can build up to a level where you (pardon the pun) flip your lid. But regular toggling of the release valve of anger can be healthy and productive in the course of grief work.

While this is fairly conventional wisdom, people in the midst of grief can sometimes miss the obvious. In other aspects of living, we all know that if we don't deal with our anger in healthy, constructive ways, our anger ends up dealing with us. The pressure of unreleased anger is physically, emotionally, and spiritually damaging. Consider this:

> The constant flood of stress chemicals and associated metabolic changes that accompany recurrent unmanaged anger can eventually cause harm to many different systems of the body. Some of the short and long-term health problems that have been linked to unmanaged anger include:
>
> Headache
> Digestion problems, such as abdominal pain
> Insomnia
> Increased anxiety
> Depression
> High blood pressure
> Skin problems, such as eczema
> Heart attack
> Stroke
> (BetterHealthChannel.com Sept. 21, 2009)

Grief carries its own physical consequences and when compounded by unexpressed anger it can truly take a tremendous toll on the body.

But when we are in the depth of grief, it is sometimes hard to see the obvious. We dismiss the physical consequences of our unexpressed anger because we simply can't bear to admit that we are angry! Hurt, sad, numb, yes, but angry? That is too hard.

Anger is defined as "a strong feeling of annoyance, displeasure, or hostility." It is much too difficult to climb up from the depths of our sorrow to acknowledge feelings like annoyance displeasure and especially hostility.

One of the main reasons that we don't acknowledge our anger while grieving the loss of a loved one is because our emotionally exhausted souls simply can't handle the negative emotion that has sent us straight into denial about our anger—namely guilt. Many grieving people realize they are experiencing symptoms of anger, allowing for the fleeting feeling of "I am so mad that I am alone," "How could my father leave me at a time like this,"? "I am angry that my husband died and left me to do all this," "Why didn't she take better care of herself," etc., and then immediately feel guilty that they are feeling that way! And so we stuff down the anger we feel toward our loved one for dying so that we don't have to feel guilty about being mad.

But consider this; anger is part of who God created us to be. All of our emotions, all of our psychological make-up are part of His great design. As He knit you together in your mother's womb and even as He breathed creation into being, anger was part of His choice for who we are and how we are to function. Our emotions, ALL of our emotions, are a gift from Him: joy, love, happiness, sadness, guilt, ennui, and yes, even anger.

The scriptures give us understanding of this God-given emotion, and even give us permission to be honest in acknowledging that yes, I am mad that somebody died and left me.

Probably the most recognized story of anger in the Bible is the passage where Jesus threw the moneylenders off the temple steps. His anger was well deserved. He has just entered Jerusalem to face the final week of his life. It is the week of Passover, and many religious pilgrims from the surrounding countryside have traveled a long way to the Temple.

As Jesus enters the sacred temple He discovers that people have set up tables for the exchange of currency and to sell doves for ritual sacrifice in the temple. Matthew 21 tells it this way:

> *Jesus entered the temple area and drove out all who were buying and selling there. He overturned the tables of the money changers and the benches of those selling doves. "It is written," he said the them, "My house will be called a house of prayer, but you are making it a den of robbers." (Matthew 21:12-13, NIV 1984)*

He sets a perfect example of anger acknowledged, anger expressed and anger directed toward the source.

The Old Testament describes many accounts of God's anger against his creation. Again and again, the nation of Israel repeatedly abandoned Him and walked away from his commandments. Again and again, with the consistency of human stubbornness, they insisted on seeking their own way. And God responded in anger acknowledging, expressing and directing this legitimate and reasonable reaction. Because God is God His anger was expressed in many ways; words, floods, broken tablets, etc. In other words, God is able to express anger in ways that are unavailable to us. Fortunately we are confined to just words, which are a good thing; imagine if you had the power to flood the earth every time you got mad! But the point is, we are made in His image, and anger is part of our created being.

In the following passage from Numbers 11, we see God acknowledging, expressing and directing His anger against the Israelites. He has safely delivered them from oppression and slavery in Egypt. He has miraculously brought them through the Red Sea and swallowed Pharaoh's army in high waves of water to ensure their safe passage; He has a plan for their nation and a history of providing for them. Yet they turn away and we see an angry God:

Numbers 11

> *Now the people complained about their hardships in the hearing of the LORD, and when he heard them his anger was aroused. Then fire from the LORD burned among them and consumed some of the outskirts of the camp. When the people cried out to Moses, he prayed to the LORD and the fire died down. So that place was called Taberah, because fire from the LORD had burned among them.*

Notice that Moses' response is to pray, and his prayers are effective in releasing the intensity of God's anger against the people.

> *The rabble with them began to crave other food, and again the Israelites started wailing and said, "If only we had meat to eat! We remember the fish we ate in Egypt at no cost—also the cucumbers, melons, leeks, onions and garlic. But now we have lost our appetite; we never see anything but this manna!" The manna was like coriander seed and looked like resin. The people went around gathering it, and then ground it in a handmill or crushed it in a mortar. They cooked it in a pot or made it into cakes. And it tasted like something made with olive oil. When the dew settled on the camp at night, the manna also came down. Moses heard the people of every family wailing, each at the entrance to his tent. The LORD became exceedingly angry, and Moses was troubled.*

And so we see God feeling anger that the provision of His plan and His design for their freedom and future is being outright rejected as the people long to return to slavery for the price of a piece of meat. And Moses, too, responds in anger;

> He asked the LORD, "Why have you brought this trouble on your servant? What have I done to displease you that you put the burden of all these people on me? Did I conceive all these people? Did I give them birth? Why do you tell me to carry them in my arms, as a nurse carries an infant, to the land you promised on oath to their forefathers? Where can I get meat for all these people? They keep wailing to me, 'Give us meat to eat!' I cannot carry all these people by myself; the burden is too heavy for me. If this is how you are going to treat me, put me to death right now—if I have found favor in your eyes—and do not let me face my own ruin."

Anger acknowledged, anger expressed, anger directed. It's important that we observe Moses here, for the same outlet is provided to us. We have won the privilege by the blood of the cross to approach God with all of our 'stuff.' Yes, he loves us that much. He loves us as much as He loved Moses, and so it is all right to go before him and say "I am mad. I don't deserve this. I didn't bring this on. If this is how you're going to treat me, put me to death!"

Here is the good news, friends. God is bigger than your anger.

God is bigger than your anger even when you are angry with *Him*. Being angry with God is actually a natural and common response to death. People of faith believe in the power God has to heal and save. People of faith have read and studied Jesus' miracles. We've seen him cure illness, make blind people see, and even resurrect the dead. We believe! We know He can save us. And so when healing doesn't come in spite of our fervent prayers and our steadfast belief, we feel *betrayed*. Doubt and disbelief replace faith, and we are stunned to realize our Lord, in whom we have put all our hope, has betrayed us. Like Job, we only know the suffering that a silent God can bring. And that makes us angry.

See what God does for Moses, after Moses honestly toggles his anger, releasing all of its pressure full blast to the One who can handle it:

> *The LORD said to Moses: "Bring me seventy of Israel's elders who are known to you as leaders and officials among the people. Have them come to the Tent of Meeting, that they may stand there with you. I will come down and speak with you there, and I will take of the Spirit that is on you and put the Spirit on them. They will help you carry the burden of the people so that you will not have to carry it alone". (Numbers 11:1-16, NIV1984)*

Do you see it? He provides. He doesn't meet honest anger with anger, but immediately comes along side of you with support, help and hope. And often, as in the case of Moses above, He will meet your honest anger by calling others to come alongside of you to carry the burden of your grief so that you will not have to carry it alone. He knows you can't carry it all by yourself; He knows the burden is too heavy.

And consider also that God in His omnipotence knows better than we do what is best for us. Our thoughts are not His thoughts and He sees things through the lens of eternity when we focus on the here and now. Mary and Martha experience this when Lazarus falls ill. They immediately send for Jesus because with a blink of an eye, Jesus can heal their brother. They've seen him do it; they believe. But Jesus doesn't come. One day passes, two days pass, and Jesus doesn't come.

John 11

> *Now a man named Lazarus was sick. He was from Bethany, the village of Mary and her sister Martha. This Mary, whose brother Lazarus now lay sick, was the same one who poured perfume on the Lord and wiped his feet with her hair. So the sisters sent word to Jesus, "Lord, the one you love is sick." When he heard this, Jesus said, "This sickness will not end in death. No, it is for God's glory so that God's Son may be glorified through it." Jesus loved Martha and her sister and Lazarus. Yet when he heard that Lazarus was sick, he stayed where he was two more days. Then he said to his disciples, "Let us go back to Judea." "But Rabbi," they said, "a short while ago the Jews tried to stone you, and yet you are going back there?" Jesus answered, "Are there not twelve hours of daylight? A man who walks by day will not stumble, for he sees by this world's light. It is when he walks by night that he stumbles, for he has no light." After he had said this, he went on to tell them, "Our friend Lazarus has fallen asleep; but I am going there to wake him up." His disciples replied, "Lord, if he sleeps, he will get better." Jesus had been speaking of his death, but his disciples thought he meant natural sleep. So then he told them plainly, "Lazarus is dead, and for your sake I am glad I was not there, so that you may believe. But let us go to him.*

Mary and Martha have different responses to their grief (sound familiar?). Lazarus is dead because Jesus has not come.

> *On his arrival, Jesus found that Lazarus had already been in the tomb for four days. Bethany was less than two miles from Jerusalem, and many Jews had come to Martha and Mary to comfort them in the loss of their brother. When Martha heard that Jesus was coming, she went out to meet him, but Mary stayed at home.*

Why doesn't Mary go to meet Jesus? Surely she was overcome by her grief, but she also may be quite angry with him for not arriving in time to heal her brother. When He sends word back that He specifically wants to see her (in other words, He calls her out!), listen to what she says to Him:

> ….*Martha went back and called her sister Mary aside. "The Teacher is here," she said, "and is asking for you." When Mary heard this, she got up quickly and went to him. Now Jesus had not yet entered the village, but was still at the place where Martha had met him. When the Jews who had been with Mary in the house, comforting her, noticed how quickly she got up and went out, they followed her, supposing she was going to the tomb to mourn there. When Mary reached the place where Jesus was and saw him, she fell at his feet and said, "Lord, if you had been here, my brother would not have died."*

Even though her reverence for Him causes her to fall at His feet, her words are accusatory. Anger acknowledged, anger expressed, anger directed. She is able to express her feelings because she trusts His love for her. Do you? Do you trust God's love for you? Do you understand that God loves you enough to withstand your anger? And so the story ends;

> *When Jesus saw her weeping, and the Jews who had come along with her also weeping, he was deeply moved in spirit and troubled. "Where have you laid him?" he asked. "Come and see, Lord," they replied. Jesus wept. Then the Jews said, "See how he loved him!" But some of them said, "Could not he who opened the eyes of the blind man have kept this man from dying?"*

Is this the question that burns in your heart as well? Do you find yourself making the same accusatory statements to your Lord, asking

Him why if he could restore sight to the blind, heal the sick, raise the dead, did he not keep your loved one from dying?

> *Jesus, once more deeply moved, came to the tomb. It was a cave with a stone laid across the entrance. "Take away the stone," he said. "But, Lord," said Martha, the sister of the dead man, "by this time there is a bad odor, for he has been there four days." Then Jesus said, "Did I not tell you that if you believed, you would see the glory of God?"*

This helps us to know that in our grief, Jesus weeps. In our grief, Jesus is deeply moved and troubled by our sorrow. In our grief, we are never alone. And the good news is that Jesus has the power to reveal the glory of God to us, even through the death of our loved one.

> *So they took away the stone. Then Jesus looked up and said, "Father, I thank you that you have heard me. I knew that you always hear me, but I said this for the benefit of the people standing here, that they may believe that you sent me." When he had said this, Jesus called in a loud voice, "Lazarus, come out!" The dead man came out, his hands and feet wrapped with strips of linen, and a cloth around his face. Jesus said to them, "Take off the grave clothes and let him go." (John 11:1-44, NIV1984)*

The lesson here is that it's okay to be angry. But it's not okay to *stay* angry. Mostly it's not okay to stay angry because of what it does to you. So toggle your anger. Stick a fork in the release valve in a productive healthy way and let off some steam. Reduce the pressure and acknowledge that anger is God's gift to us so that stress won't result in our heads blowing off. Find empathetic friends, go for a run, join a support group, call your clergy person; find some healthy way to let it out. Take some time and retreat from your daily obligations to be alone with Him for that process of releasing the pressure of your anger.

Begin by acknowledging your anger by saying first to yourself, "I am mad." Next find a way to express it to someone else by exploring aspects of your anger. Express the specific things that are making you mad. Call a friend or pastor and say out loud "I am so angry to have to do all the bills by myself." "It makes me mad that I now have to cook all my meals alone." "I am so mad that she ignored my pleas to stop drinking and driving?" "I'm angry that he didn't get regular checkups like I told him." "It really bothers me to be alone in the evening." And finally, direct your anger to the source through journaling or praying. Write a letter to your loved one and place it on the grave. Go to an altar and pray an angry prayer; climb up a hill or sand dune and shake your fist at God!

Friends, anger is part of God's design; it is a gift of normal, regular emotion and an important step in your healing when you release it. If you release your anger to Him, you will find that He has the manna that will soothe your hurt and sustain your soul. When we take the grave clothes off our anger and acknowledge the power of God, we encounter the peace that comes from Him and Him alone. And remember that Jesus is the Resurrection and the Life, and it is on this that we build our hope.

CHAPTER TWO

Becky

Becky always loved to work on puzzles when she was a child. She remembers spending countless hours putting pieces together during fun-filled family vacations. Some proved more challenging than others, but most contained hundreds of little pieces that were so separate and distinct—Becky loved how each piece played its own part in creating the bigger, more beautiful picture that came to life when the puzzle was completed. What Becky didn't realize then was how those puzzles would come to teach her a lesson that God had in store for her life.

Growing up in Lancaster, Ohio, Becky loved living in the country with her mom, dad, and younger brother Ben. She thinks back to those days and recalls, *We were a very close family—we did a lot together. My mom and dad raised us in a great house. We shared everything and talked all the time.* These are memories that Becky wishes she could bottle up and freeze in time. Her dad, Max, had grown up hunting and camping and he loved animals. There were always animals or parts of them around their house. "When we moved out in the country, Dad went to work for a local school as a biology teacher. He would often take my brother, Ben and me to his classroom and show us the dead animals in jars of formaldehyde," Becky says. "In the summer, Dad would bring home a few live creatures from his classroom. We always had animals around like dogs, cats, and turtles."

Living in the country also afforded them access to simple pleasures like the little fishing hole down the dirt road from their house that was teeming with sunfish. Becky's family raised Bassett Hounds with their sad brown eyes and velvety long ears. There always seemed to be puppies around their household to love and each was given a name. The time seemed to come too quickly when they would have to say good-bye as each puppy was sold. Becky loved caring for the puppies, and she also loved caring for her younger brother.

Ben was 3 1/2 years younger than Becky, and she became very protective of him in a motherly way as they grew up together. She was not just his playmate—she was also his guardian. He had one of those great imaginations that took him to faraway lands and make-believe places. In his creative play, the wooden picnic table in their backyard became a fishing boat and the acre of grassy plains became his vast blue ocean prime for fishing. Unlike Becky, who enjoyed the solitary play of puzzle making, Ben was the type of kid who needed to be around other people—he simply loved attention. Thirsting for companionship, Ben would conjure up ways to engage Becky in his world of make-believe and boyish games. But Becky would always win, persuading him to play her favorites, usually involving dressing up in girlie outfits with coordinating handbags and the engaging in the sipping of tea. Unlike typical siblings, Becky and Ben never fought. Their mom attributed that to Becky's easy-going nature. Becky and Ben would later become best friends.

"Christmas was really special for us," says Becky. "My mom always made it fun. She would take pictures every year of Ben and me coming down the stairs in our pajamas. It was hysterical because I had these cute pink fuzzy robes, and my mom would hand them down to my little brother, who thought nothing of it. So we had these pictures of Ben in my old robe, and we're smiling as we look down at the Christmas tree. We had a great time!" Joy-filled memories like playing dress-up, fishing at the little hole and Christmastime spent together would become very precious to Becky.

The family all gathered together one Friday evening, May 20, 1988, to celebrate the birth of Becky's first child. It would be a time of family fellowship and great fun, but it would also be the last time the family would see Ben alive.

Heading to work Monday morning, May 23, 1988, Ben made a decision about his route that would cost him his life. Intense fog and pouring rain hampered his visibility from all sides, so Ben chose the country roads instead of the highway because he had driven them so often. No one will ever know the exact details of how the accident happened. It was assumed that fog clouded Ben's vision as he drove down a portion of the country dirt road heading into a valley near the creek. He must have missed the one-way stop sign at the bottom of the hill just covered with new gravel. A grey pick-up truck legally travelling through the intersection hit Ben's driver's side door hurling Ben's car airborne down by the creek. Ben was thrown from the car; his body laid by the water. A neighbor, startled by what she called a loud bomb-like explosion, called 911 and rushed outside to investigate. She saw Ben and ran to him, and like a prophet straight out of the Bible, she kneeled down gently by his side, took rainwater in her hand and baptized him, staying by his side until authorities arrived. Unfortunately, Ben did not survive the impact of the crash.

The day following the accident, Becky's husband Dan visited the crash site to rummage through debris looking for Ben's personal belongings. Items were scattered everywhere, and as Dan began carefully picking through the grass by the creek, a woman approached him. She was the neighbor who had heard the crash and stayed with Ben. It was important for her to share with Ben's family what transpired while she sat with Ben there by the creek. She told Dan of her great assurance that Ben was with God, because she felt his soul leave the body and sensed the most amazing connection with him. She was anxious to find the family and give them peace that Ben was okay now in his heavenly home.

Becky found that first year after Ben's death to be painfully difficult. Ben was her best friend, the one she phoned to share her day with and the one she leaned on whenever she had a problem. Recalling that initial period following Ben's death Becky says, "Life becomes something to get through—let's get through the first five minutes, ten minutes; we got through a day, one more day; we got through a week, a month. Then it becomes events that you have to get through as well. You survive the first birthday without him, the first Mother's Day, Father's Day, Easter and Christmas."

That first Christmas after Ben's death the entire family, including Ben's widow, Helen, daughter Elizabeth and newborn son Nathan, gathered together at Becky's parents' house to spend the night. "On Christmas Eve we lit a candle in memory of Ben," Becky says. "However, nothing makes it easier. The first year you just survive it and pat yourself on the back for getting through it. The second year is still really hard; after the fifth year you realize that life has gone on."

"Whether you like it or not, when you go through grief, all of a sudden you become someone people come to for advice—like you're an expert on the grief process," Becky says. She struggled with how to provide the insight people wanted from her about how to move through the process and begin living again. Then it hit her—all those countless hours spent manipulating tiny puzzle pieces into their correct places when she was younger came into focus. The response to "How do you go on living when someone you loved dies?" was hidden in her puzzles. Becky explains, "Life is like a puzzle. There are all these pieces that create the puzzle picture, and then this one big piece is removed—a big part of the puzzle. Special parts of the picture are on this piece, and no matter what you do you just can't put another piece in its place—it simply won't fit. Now you have this hole in your puzzle, and nothing can fill that hole. So how do you go forward from here? You will go on and should go on because if you don't, what kind of tribute is that to the person who died? What does that say? I know what my brother would say. Ben would tell me that he would feel sad knowing that I was not going on with my life, having children, and enjoying myself, all because he lost his life in a car crash."

Becky had an immense faith and handed her grief over to the Lord praying things like "How do I go on enjoying life? Where do I go from here? How can I keep Ben's memory alive? And, how do I make something really good out of something bad?" With His perfect timing God answered Becky's prayers in a big way, as if creating His own masterpiece puzzle—piece by piece.

In school, Becky remembers how she loved English composition and writing. It was something that came very naturally to her, but she was inexperienced at doing any type of professional writing. However, when she was approached by Fairview Christian Church in Ohio and asked to develop a family worship and large-group children's program, Becky and her husband, Dan seized the opportunity to use her creative imagination. The church provided Becky with generic puppets, leaving her to decide the characters' identities and personalities. Despite her inexperience at writing children's church curriculum, Becky dove in and decided to create the puppets as kids, because she felt that kids could learn through others "kids" their age who shared the same types of experiences. Becky made a point to really listen and watch what kids around her were going through, eventually leading her to the idea of creating a puppet show each week with situations similar to those on television. Her format would include the kid puppet characters trying to deal with problems—real-life problems—who would turn to the Bible for answers, or to God, or to an authority figure in the church. This approach would create a relaxed, non-threatening environment where kids would learn about God without even realizing it. "We found out that a lot of what we enjoyed and found funny the kids also found funny," Becky says. *I can write these—I can do this*, she thought.

Becky was very intentional about how she approached this ministry. "In the beginning, what we did was go to the kids' world and then take them to the world of puppet make-believe, and we found in these pilot episodes that it was working," Becky says. It started with two puppets—a little boy Stuart, based on her brother, Ben, and his older sister, Sally, based on Becky. The weekly puppet shows became a family affair as Becky's sons Curtis and Hunter jumped in to play additional parts.

It became clear to Becky that this puppet ministry was more than just volunteer work: it was the answer to prayer she had hoped would have come overnight, but that actually took many years to take shape. Since Ben's death, Becky had been faithfully praying to God for some way to make sense of Ben's passing. And now she realized He was in the process of answering her all along, and it felt good.

Through the writing and performing of the puppet shows, Becky was reliving her fun-filled childhood memories. Her personality and that of her brother were coming out in these two little puppet characters. "It was an amazing time for me—a time of healing, because I was able to use my personal experiences (my life with Ben, my love of writing, and the puppets) to touch the lives of children in my church. I realized that only in ministry would I have been given this opportunity, and I knew from then on I was never going to be able to do anything else," she says.

Success came with its challenges though—like convincing her audience that puppets were not "old school." "Children and adults love to watch The Muppet Show, which has had phenomenal success," Becky says. "Kermit is Kermit—Kermit is not a puppet. Our goal was always to make Stuart and Sally seem real, because if we could do that, then they would become more believable through their dialogue and their interactions and the children could relate to them. It wasn't about how expensive the puppets were, because you can spend thousands of dollars on a puppet but kids won't necessarily want to watch it. You can put a simple flip top puppet like Stuart up there with that stupid orange hair doing dumb stuff, saying funny things, arguing with Sally, and they're just Stuart and Sally." Every goal Becky set she achieved, but she knew she achieved it because God was blessing her and still working on the masterpiece puzzle of her life. Everything Becky attempted in ministry seemed to be a stepping-stone for the next part, which was yet to be revealed.

God wasn't finished with Becky's life puzzle yet; He still had more pieces to fit together. God continued to provide blessings for Becky, demonstrating that He had not forsaken her, and teaching her that the loss of a loved one doesn't have to mean the end. The large group ministry that Becky created would eventually make it to television, winning an award for "Best Children's Special in 1999." "It was an amazing time in my life, because I felt like I was being paid to learn and grow again," she says. "I didn't know why this was all happening, but I had to trust that God did."

The doors kept opening, and Becky and her family decided to travel on their own, using the puppet shows as an outreach ministry. They witnessed its success in a church setting and a television setting, but when they realized it was portable, the sky was the limit—they could go anywhere.

However, when things seemed to be going so well, unexpected news came that Dan's brother, Perry, was diagnosed with small cell lymphoma. Dan owned a business with Perry and wanted to move close to him to support his brother and help out with the business. So Dan and Becky left Ohio and arrived in Atlanta, Georgia, in 2001—seven months before Perry lost his fight with cancer. "Perry fought cancer for seven years and died at the age of forty-six, so Dan and I both lost brothers," Becky says. "A lot of people thought we would go back to Ohio, but we didn't. I started working in children's ministry in the Atlanta area, trying to be creative and continuing to use the puppets." By now Becky had four main copyrighted puppets: Stuart, Sally, Josie and Stan, as well as several others. Puppets will always be a part of Becky's life. "I would like to take puppets to a hospital at some point. That would be cool because they don't have that in hospitals today," Becky says. Her idea would be to create puppets with no hair, puppets in wheelchairs, and puppets with cancer and other illnesses; they would be real kids in real situations.

Today Becky is the director of a vibrant and effective Children's Ministry at a large church south of Atlanta where she coordinates weekly kid-oriented large group programming incorporating drama, dancing, singing and a little humor to teach children about Jesus Christ. Hundreds of kids and their families attend each week.

Becky looks back and reflects on God's amazing hand at work in her life. God gifted her with talents and used all the experiences in her life to bring something good out of her loss. She thinks back on the amazing journey. *God doesn't answer prayer overnight because sometimes the lessons can only be learned through the journey. I could never have learned this in school, and I'm so thankful it worked out the way it did because I don't think I would have been ready to do this earlier in my life. I couldn't have appreciated it as much. I still would like to have my brother here—he would have enjoyed it. I think he is here.*

"So much has transpired," she says. "Stuart and Sally started back in 1994—actually, way back in 1960 and 1964 when Ben and I were born. So I feel like God has allowed me to make something good out of something bad, even though I didn't know at the time what that "something good" would be. It's been an unbelievable, God-inspired journey that began in 1994 and is still going. What else could I have done with my life that would have been a better tribute to my amazing brother Ben?"

Omniscience
Rev. Haas

One of our favorite vacation activities is puzzle making. There are stacks of one thousand- piece puzzles in the beach cottage we rent every summer, and we have probably made each one four or five times over the years. Our daughter Sarah is a puzzle fanatic and is our starter. Sarah meticulously searches the box for the 'edge pieces' and lays them all out on the coffee table before beginning. Once each one has been found, she then quickly and deftly assembles the frame of the puzzle by matching the edges. We have learned to wait until this process is complete before joining in; Sarah is our puzzle master. Over the next few days we all work on the puzzle, putting it together piece by piece as we wait for our turn for the shower, watch a movie together, wait for the last one to be ready to leave for the restaurant, etc. Sarah is the most focused and diligent, and it is not uncommon for her to stay up till the wee hours of morning when a puzzle is nearing completion.

As a puzzle master, Sarah will not look at the picture on the lid of the box. The rest of the family is constantly checking progress of the puzzle against the picture, looking for visual clues about what comes next, what fits where. But Sarah watches shapes and pieces, allowing the picture to unfold as she faithfully fits interlocking piece with interlocking piece. I asked her once why she didn't look at the picture on the lid, and she explained simply that she sees the picture one time when she opens the box and from that point it's just a matter of paying attention to make sure each piece finds its own place. She likes to wait until the puzzle is complete before she sees the picture again; that's the reward for the hard work of piecing everything together, and the only way the picture makes sense to her. The picture can only be seen when all the pieces are in their proper place.

One of the more difficult aspects of loss and the grief that follows it is the futile attempt we make to try to make sense out of what has happened. Our minds are constantly trying to work the puzzle out. Why did he die? What is the reason she is gone? How can this have happened? Is this really my life?

Unbidden, our thoughts go back to the death over and over and over again, replaying the events of the loss until we are literally sick of our thoughts. And then we replay it again. It reminds me of one summer vacation when the heat index had climbed to 107 degrees, forcing us to remain inside in the cool. Luckily for us, there was a "Little House on the Prairie" marathon on television (and a puzzle to do!). Unluckily for us, the station programmer had made a mistake and every commercial break showed the same Betty Crocker Scalloped Potato commercial. If the break allowed for three commercials, it played three times in a row. Next commercial break, it was the same exact commercial, over and over and over. "Betty Crocker knows…. what guys want." Have mercy! To phrase it like our southern friends, it began work our last nerve in a hurry and as the second "Little House" episode began to air, we switched to a movie on videotape. We just couldn't take the mindless repetition of the same words and images over and over and over.

Unfortunately we don't have the same option when it comes to grief recovery. We just can't shut it down and put in a new tape. It takes time, it takes support, it takes courage and it takes faith. Most of all, it takes perseverance to put the puzzle pieces together, one piece at a time, before we can see the entire picture of our life without our loved one coming together. The reason we can't see the picture before the process is complete is because we don't have access to the lid of the box.

But here's the good news; God does.

In fancy theological language, we say that God is omniscient. This is to say that God is all-knowing; He sees everything and understands everything. Not only does He see the lid of the box, He created it. He is patiently standing over our shoulder watching as we methodically put the pieces of our lives together. We refer to God's presence as 'omnipresence' in theological terms (meaning that God is always and constantly present everywhere), and this understanding is a comfort and a source of encouragement. Consider this passage from Psalms:

Psalm 33

1 Sing joyfully to the LORD, you righteous; it is fitting for the upright to praise him.

2 Praise the LORD with the harp; make music to him on the ten-stringed lyre.

3 Sing to him a new song; play skillfully, and shout for joy.

4 For the word of the LORD is right and true; he is faithful in all he does.

5 The LORD loves righteousness and justice; the earth is full of his unfailing love.

6 By the word of the LORD were the heavens made, their starry host by the breath of his mouth.

7 He gathers the waters of the sea into jars; he puts the deep into storehouses.

8 Let all the earth fear the LORD; let all the people of the world revere him.

9 For he spoke, and it came to be; he commanded, and it stood firm.

10 The LORD foils the plans of the nations; he thwarts the purposes of the peoples.

11 But the plans of the LORD stand firm forever, the purposes of his heart through all generations.

12 Blessed is the nation whose God is the LORD, the people he chose for his inheritance.

13 From heaven the LORD looks down and sees all mankind;

14 from his dwelling place he watches all who live on earth—

15 he who forms the hearts of all, who considers everything they do.

16 No king is saved by the size of his army; no warrior escapes by his great strength.

17 A horse is a vain hope for deliverance; despite all its great strength it cannot save.

18 But the eyes of the LORD are on those who fear him, on those whose hope is in his unfailing love,

19 to deliver them from death and keep them alive in famine.

20 We wait in hope for the LORD; he is our help and our shield.

21 In him our hearts rejoice, for we trust in his holy name.

22 May your unfailing love rest upon us, O LORD, even as we put our hope in you. (Psalm 33:1-22, NIV1984)

What beautiful words! The Psalmist is describing His omniscient and omnipresent God who has given him unfailing love and hope. What comfort it brings the broken-hearted to know that God is ever vigilant in watching us in our mourning. God knows. "From heaven the LORD looks down and sees all mankind; from his dwelling place he watches all who live on earth—he who forms the hearts of all, who considers everything they do." He sees our tears, and he knows the depth of our suffering.

One aspect of the Lord's omniscience is His ability to know our feelings. He knew where to hang the sun, and He knows what is in your heart when you are hanging your head in agony. He knew where to place the stars and He knows the place that sadness has in your heart this very moment. Just as He spun the earth on its axis to set life into motion, He knows how to heal your wound and spin your lifeless life into motion again.

Do you know the New Testament story of the Paralytic?

The Gospel According to Luke tells the story of four faithful friends who bring their paralyzed friend to a home where Jesus is conducting a lesson. When they arrive, they discover that there is such a crowd in front of the door they can't get in:

Luke 5:17-26

> *One day as he was teaching, Pharisees and teachers of the law, who had come from every village of Galilee and from Judea and Jerusalem, were sitting there. And the power of the Lord was present for him to heal the sick. Some men came carrying*

a paralytic on a mat and tried to take him into the house to lay him before Jesus. When they could not find a way to do this because of the crowd, they went up on the roof and lowered him on his mat through the tiles into the middle of the crowd, right in front of Jesus.

Jesus is undisturbed by the interruption. Imagine what would happen if in the middle of your next Bible study, somebody dropped a guy down in front of the class on a mat through a hole in the roof! But Jesus is not surprised, having known of their presence. He simply responds about the quality of their faith;

When Jesus saw their faith, he said, "Friend, your sins are forgiven."

But what happens next is truly amazing. The Pharisees begin to think negative thoughts about what Jesus has just done. *And Jesus knows what they are thinking.*

The Pharisees and the teachers of the law began thinking to themselves, "Who is this fellow who speaks blasphemy? Who can forgive sins but God alone?" Jesus knew what they were thinking and asked, "Why are you thinking these things in your hearts? Which is easier: to say, 'Your sins are forgiven,' or to say, 'Get up and walk'"?

Saving the best for last, Jesus now does the unbelievable. He heals the man by the power of His word.

But that you may know that the Son of Man has authority on earth to forgive sins...." He said to the paralyzed man, "I tell you, get up, take your mat and go home." Immediately he stood up in front of them, took what he had been lying on and went home praising God. Everyone was amazed and gave praise to God.

They were filled with awe and said, "We have seen remarkable
things today." (Luke 5:17-26, NIV1984)

What did Jesus know? He knew the paralyzed man was there. He
knew what other men were thinking. He knew the quality of their
faith. He knew how to forgive sins. And he knew how to heal the
man's paralysis.

Many people in the midst of grief feel paralyzed. They are unable to
feel joy, excitement, anticipation or engagement. This phase is a state
of emotional numbness and it is quite common after a significant loss.
Perhaps it is the heart's way of preventing further injury; 'If I care
less, it can't hurt more.' I remember hearing a friend's mother tell her
sons upon the death of their father; "If it hadn't been so good, this
wouldn't hurt so bad." So somehow in defense of hurt, we allow our
emotions to become paralyzed, trying to insulate ourselves from the
real world and all its trials.

Or to put it more eloquently, hear this exchange between a young girl
named Lily, and grown up but emotionally fragile Miss May from
"The Secret Life of Bees":

> *Lily: "Miss May I know you get real sad sometimes. My daddy*
> *never feels….he never felt….anything. I'd rather be like you."*

> *Miss May: "The worker bee weighs less than the flower petal.*
> *But she can fly with a load heavier than her. But she only lives*
> *four or five weeks. Sometimes not feeling is the only way you can*
> *survive." (Sue Monk Kidd, The Secret Life of Bees)*

Sometimes, not feeling is the only way you can survive. But mere
survival isn't God's plan. Jesus came that you might have life, and
have it abundantly. So while survival wrought from numbness may

be necessary in the short term, it cannot sustain real, abundant life in the long term. Jesus tells us:

John 10

> *The thief comes only in order to steal and kill and destroy. I came that they may have and enjoy life, and have it in abundance (to the full, till it overflows). (John 10:10, Amplified Bible)*

You see, the problem with paralysis is that while it insulates us from hurt, it also insulates us from happiness. The thing we lack, i.e. joy, is the thing we need the most and yet our numbness makes it unattainable to us. The joy that would lift us up is the price we pay in a futile effort to not hurt so much, making the antidote we desperately need just out of our reach.

Jesus knows that you are there. He knows what you are thinking, feeling, and not feeling. He knows the quality of your faith. And if your faith is weak, He knows ways to strengthen it. He knows how to forgive your sins, and if your sins are many, repentance is available to cleanse you of them. Best of all, He knows how to heal your grief. He will do it in His time if you will let Him. He will accomplish it with you doing a lot of hard work.

Consider that God, too, suffered as he watched His only Son die on a cross. He also knew what it was like to be separated from someone He loved, if only for a short while. Scriptures tell us that on the day of the crucifixion, the earth went completely black the moment that Jesus died. His body was removed and encased in a shroud and placed in a temporary tomb. A huge stone was rolled in front of the entrance of the tomb, and on the third day the women came to prepare his body for permanent burial. But He was not there.

The early Christian church fathers understood the three-day period between Christ's death and resurrection to be a time when He "descended into Hell," having taken the sins of the world upon Him. These are the words of the Roman Catholic Apostle's Creed:

1. I believe in God, the Father almighty, creator of heaven and earth.

2. I believe in Jesus Christ, his only Son, our Lord.

3. He was conceived by the power of the Holy Spirit and born of the Virgin Mary.

4. He suffered under Pontius Pilate, was crucified, died, and was buried.

5. *He descended into hell. On the third day he rose again.*

6. He ascended into heaven and is seated at the right hand of the Father.

7. He will come again to judge the living and the dead.

8. I believe in the Holy Spirit,

9. the holy catholic Church, the communion of saints,

10. the forgiveness of sins,

11. the resurrection of the body,

12. and the life everlasting. Amen

(Peter J. Vaghi, The Faith We Profess: A Catholic Guide to the Apostles' Creed (Notre Dame, IN: Ave Maria Press, 2008),4.)

Even in the very definition of the word sin, i.e. "separation from God," we can see that Christ's taking on of our sins was a time of complete separation from God, until three days had passed and He accomplished the resurrection. During that time, God was like us in our grieving—alone, separated by the distance that death imposes, experiencing loneliness and sadness. Has anyone approached you and said, "I know exactly how you feel," and in your head you respond, "No you don't. You can't possibly have a clue about how I feel."? Well, guess what; God knows exactly how you feel.

Hear this now, for this is the good news for all who believe. Because of the resurrection, Son and Father were reunited. Because of the resurrection, we all will be reunited with our loved ones for eternity.

> *"For God so loved the world that he gave his only begotten Son that whosoever believeth in him SHALL NOT PERISH but have everlasting life." (John 3:16, King James Version)*

Thus the final piece of the puzzle fits into place and the picture comes together in a cohesive whole. It is a picture of hope, built on the promise of the resurrection. As the old hymn says:

> My hope is built on nothing less than Jesus' blood and righteousness.

> I dare not trust the sweetest frame but wholly lean on Jesus' name.

> On Christ the solid rock I stand; all other ground is sinking sand.

> All other ground is sinking sand. (William Bradbury, 1863)

So while you wait, try to become a disciplined puzzle-maker. Be like the puzzle-master who resists the temptation to try to look at the picture on the lid of the box and instead, allow God in His time to reveal the picture to you. Remember that success comes in working hard at just putting each puzzle piece in its place. Does it bring you comfort to realize that each tear, each sleepless night, each mournful thought, is just another interlocking piece finding its place in the big picture?

Do the work of your grief recovery with great intention and energy. Be deliberate in rejecting the playback of your loved one's death again and again from your mind, filling your mind instead with good things like happy memories, the support of friends, the making of new memories or reading the Psalms every time you begin to feel your thoughts slip that way. Remember that while you are not all-knowing, you are loved by the One who is and He is here. He is in charge of your picture, and His plan is to give you a future with hope. This is God's big picture for your life:

> *"For I know the plans I have for you"*, says the Lord. *"Plans to prosper you and not harm you. Plans to give you a future with HOPE."* (Jeremiah 29:11, NIV1984)

May your unfailing love rest upon us, O LORD, even as we put our hope in You.

CHAPTER THREE

Kelly

The curtain opened on the spring performance of Grease at a Christian High School in Georgia. The entire Thomas family had come to watch Mike perform; father Brian, mother Sally, sister Kelly and brother Justin. It was a family reunion of sorts, as Brian had come from his temporary home in South Dakota where he was working to support his family. At the end of the show, performers found their admiring families for hugs and handshakes in the noisy theatre lobby. After hugging brother Mike, Kelly turned to hug her father, as he would be leaving the next morning to return to his job far away. As he embraced her, she suddenly found herself clinging to him and whispering, "Don't go. Don't do it." She couldn't have known it, but that night was the last time she would ever see her Dad alive.

The Thomas home was a typical Christian home with two loving parents providing a stable foundation. Kelly describes her mother Sally as the "spiritual leader of our family" and experienced her father Brian as a loving man who had very high standards for his family. These standards led Kelly to strive very hard in sports and in her studies so as not to disappoint her father. While he never insisted on perfection, he set limits on her activities so that her grades were not affected. But Kelly says, "In my mind, if I didn't get an A, then it wasn't good enough. So I would go to the extreme. I heard "be perfect, be perfect, be perfect" in my mind over and over. Her self-imposed drive for perfection would even find its way into her relationship with

God, where she convinced herself that she had to work to be good enough to merit His favor.

Before moving to Georgia, the entire family lived in Rapid City, South Dakota where they were extremely close. Kelly explains, "In South Dakota, there's nothing to do, so everyone does sports." She grew up participating in gymnastics, volleyball, swimming, diving, dance team, and track; she was a four-sport varsity athlete. "There was this performance thing that was driving me; like I wanted to make my parents proud of me. I wanted to be the best." She longed for her parents' approval, love and time, but got little of the time she craved. Both her parents worked full time with Brian working from 7 a.m. to 7 p.m. most days. He often went to bed early, leaving little quality time for those daddy and daughter special moments.

During a routine dive practice, Kelly unexpectedly sustained neck and back injuries. Subsequent nerve issues caused her normally strong legs to give out at unexpected moments. Kelly was strongly determined to try to push through the pain and continue with sports, but an orthopedist in Rapid City ended her dream when he diagnosed her with three bulging discs in her back. The doctor admonished her to take an entire year off, and then participate in fewer sports, or she would not be able to participate in college sports. Kelly felt as though her world had collapsed. "Everything that defined my identity, and all the self worth that I had built up by proving myself in sports was gone."

After her injury, Kelly began dedicating more time to her relationship with Christ. She had been a Christian for as long as she could remember, and had accepted Christ as her Savior, but had never been baptized. After reading scripture which instructed her to believe and be baptized, she realized the time had come to take a step of obedience and trust God. In her faith system, this meant a baptism by immersion where she would share her personal testimony before the whole church.

Of her baptism, Kelly recalls, "When you get dunked, you come up out of the water and feel like you're exactly the same, but then you find that God is just beginning to work with you." During this time, Kelly's parents were also growing stronger in their faith and made the decision to move to Georgia. The move gave Kelly had a strange sense of peace about her injury situation. "Even though sports had been such an important part of my life, I felt peace and freedom knowing that if God wanted to return sports to me, he would give me that opportunity in Georgia."

The Thomas family arrived in Georgia over the next summer and Kelly was enrolled in a Christian high school as a junior. She had taken the full year of rehabilitation sessions and rest as prescribed for her back and was anxious to attend volleyball tryouts in July. "During tryouts, I was doing so well. But on the second to last day, my back started to bother me. I wasn't sure if I pulled a muscle," she says. "I sobbed silently to myself. We prayed, we iced my back, and literally the next day, it was just a little sore and I was able to play." She was able to play for the next two years. "I had surrendered playing sports back in South Dakota, and God gave that back to me."

The move to Georgia afforded Sally the opportunity to quit working full time and fulfill her dream of being a stay-at-home mom. Brian was able to work out of their home. "My parents got up, ate breakfast with us, got us ready for school and when we arrived home, they were there. All of a sudden my relationship with my parents just exploded—it blossomed! They were now my best friends and spiritual role models."

The move was also a catalyst for Brian's spiritual growth. "My Dad's relationship with God grew exponentially and literally transformed before my eyes, and through my last years in high school and then college there was a huge trust between us and I felt deep gratitude for him. I became very reliant on him."

When she left home to attend college, Kelly and her dad spoke on the phone every day. She had been turning to her dad for advice for years, yet there was one singular conversation between them that was life changing. It will remain with Kelly for the rest of her life.

Kelly had been involved in an on-again-off-again romance for two years with a young man she was certain she would marry. She sought her father out for advice one day in the sunroom of their house. She vividly recalls their talk as though it was yesterday.

Brian began, "Kelly, do you know that I love you?"

Kelly replied, "Yes, Dad, I know that you love me."

He continued, "Have I ever led you astray or told you something wrong? Can you trust me?"

Kelly answered, "Yes, Dad, I can trust you."

Her father went on, "And do you know I have your best interest at heart?"

"Yes, Dad, I do."

And then he laid out his plan. "I think you need to take the summer off from your boyfriend and not talk to each other. Take some time off from one another. By the end of the summer, you will have had enough time and enough distance between you to know what you want, and he'll know what he wants."

Kelly says, "I knew my Dad loved me, I knew he had my best interest at heart, but his advice hurt so much. I crawled up onto his lap, a big college girl, and sobbed because I knew he was right." By the end of the summer, she broke off the relationship and ended up meeting her future husband six months later.

During the time that Kelly was putting her life together, her dad's life was slowly and silently unraveling thread by slender thread. The job in Georgia proved to be far less than he had anticipated, leaving him feeling empty and unproductive. Eventually he decided to return to South Dakota for steady employment. After much discussion, the family decided that they would stay in Georgia for two years until Mike completed high school, and Brian would endure the commute.

Kelly's dad would be returning to his former hometown, where his parents and brothers still lived. Brian's brothers struggled with addictions and Kelly's grandparents relied heavily on her dad, making him feel needed back home. But returning without his wife and kids was difficult on him, and he slowly withdrew from people and life. He moved into his mother-in-law's home, and chose to live in the dark, cold basement so as not to be an imposition, even though she spent the better part of the year in Arizona.

Eventually he stopped attending church because he didn't like worshipping without his family. He began to hunt and fish on Sundays, further isolating him from the community.

He returned to Georgia to attend as many of Kelly and Mike's school events and performances as he could, and always brought gifts. Kelly was a senior in college and Mike was a high school senior. These wonderful visits always ended with heartbreaking goodbyes, and with each return to South Dakota he became more depressed. Soon he began to struggle with anxiety and insomnia. The exhausting commute began to take its toll on him.

Reading scripture only brought spiritual warfare into the situation, according to Kelly. "Satan would twist the words to condemn him. It made him feel like he was the antithesis of what the Bible was saying." He began to feel as though he was no longer an adequate provider for his family. We pleaded with him to come back to Georgia even if it meant a reduction in income. Kelly sees this as Brian slipping further into bondage—"a place that was detrimental to his emotional, physical and spiritual well-being."

Kelly was married later that same year, and when her father returned to Georgia for the wedding he had lost about 25 pounds. Kelly suspected he wasn't eating and knew he was experiencing sleep deprivation. During the wedding visit, she also noticed his hands visibly shaking and his lack of energy. Brian stirred all night and never got more than two or three hours sleep. Upon his return to South Dakota he continued to have insomnia for another three months.

During a phone call with Kelly's mother, Brian confessed that he was beginning to have dark thoughts living so far away from them. She immediately flew to South Dakota and brought him back to Georgia. Brian's boss had graciously allowed him a full month off, but only two weeks would be paid leave. Back at home with his family, he began to feel better, and so the night of Mike's performance in Grease was to be his last before returning the next morning to his job in South Dakota. Kelly knew in her heart that he wasn't ready to return, and that is why she whispered, "Don't go. Don't do it," in his ear as they embraced in the lobby that night.

Two weeks later, Kelly's father called her to share good news that his sleeping medication was helping. They discussed the family's addiction issues and Kelly cautioned her Dad about taking the pills. She would later regret this conversation because she fears it may have contributed to her father's decision to stop taking the medication.

The next day, Sally was due to fly to South Dakota for a visit, but her flight was suddenly cancelled due to a blizzard. The following morning Brian did not show up for work, and family members frantically tried reaching him by phone. Kelly's aunt finally drove over to his house and discovered to her horror that Brian had committed suicide.

Kelly's initial response to the awful news was anger. "I was very angry at God, not just for myself but for my mother. My mom's dad died of lung cancer when she was young," says Kelly. "I didn't think it was fair she also had to lose her husband, who had been her grade school sweetheart, at age 50. I was so angry and confused. How could a good God let that happen to someone who is a Christian, a spiritual leader,—someone who ministered to so many people? My Dad had been on mission trips. How could God let this happen?"

Before her father took his life, Kelly had prayed fervently that God would work out Brian's situation. She had never prayed in intercession for someone before, but found herself praying for God to restore her father and reveal what He intended for his life. But God didn't answer her prayer the way she requested, and in addition to losing her father, she was left feeling disappointed and abandoned by God.

Prior to her father's death, Kelly had two dreams about death, but she didn't know who it was. "So, I've had these weird premonitions, and suddenly as I was saying good-bye to my Dad at Mike's play I just wanted to hold onto him. Now it all made sense. "

Flying to South Dakota for the funeral, Kelly pondered what she might say during the eulogy. As she searched for the words, she suddenly heard God saying to her, "Do you know that I love you? Can you trust me? Have I ever steered you wrong?" And as her father's words returned to her in a flood, she knew what she was going to say. "I felt so strongly that God was telling me to share all my father's amazing qualities, and how Godly he was. I asked people not to be disappointed in my Dad. I told them that I was not disappointed, and that God didn't disappoint us. I spoke the truth that God put on my heart."

As the coffin was lowered into the ground at the graveside, Kelly sat in stunned silence, expecting her father to somehow miraculously rise up and come out of it. Her head was filled with thoughts like "What are you doing? You can't do that! You can't bury my father!" Kelly immediately found herself plunging into deep despair. Her mind reeled. Is God who He says He is? Does God really do what he promises? What is the purpose of faith?

For the next several months, Kelly really wrestled with her thoughts, wondering if her questioning revealed a lack of faith. She wondered if her sin would preclude God from hearing her desperate prayer for the healing of her heart. She struggled to understand why God did not answer her prayer for her father; she had always done her best at everything, and worked so hard; where was God in her most desperate hour?

A sermon series called "Faith, Hope and Luck" had been delivered to her house after the funeral, and it was while listening to the series that Kelly began to realize that her faith in God had been formed when her life's circumstances were great; when there was no strife, no sorrow, no heartache. Now her circumstances had changed drastically and suddenly her hope was gone. Her hope had been in God who could heal her father's mind; her hope had been in God who had the power to raise her father from the dead, rather than where it should be—in God healing her own heart.

"My dad always told us, 'Trust in the Lord with all your heart and lean not on your own understanding. In all your ways acknowledge Him, and he will make your path straight," says Kelly. In fact, many Bible verses that her father had spoken popped into Kelly's head. She knew it was truth, it was wisdom, and it was leading her to conclude that while she may not understand God's decisions and how something good could come out of her father's death. She would try to trust God in His time to reveal to her that goodness promised in Romans 8:28: "For God can use ALL things for the GOOD of those who love Him and are called to His purpose."

Ultimately, Kelly realized that God had always been faithful to her when she chose to believe Him. God had never let her down. At that moment, she made her decision. She prayed, "I choose You. I choose to believe You. I choose to put my hope and my faith in You. I choose to trust You even though I'm very confused about these other things like who You heal and don't heal, who You raise from the dead and who You don't raise from the dead. I choose You."

Kelly still dealt with thoughts about the way her father died, leaving no note of explanation and no indication that his suicide had been planned. Eventually she came to believe that it was Satan's influence over her father's mind that had caused him to take his life. It wasn't her Dad.

Kelly's new husband Mark helped her put a lot of this into perspective with his love, support and understanding. He shared his belief that we don't have to know all the answers—and that we may never get the answers until eternity. "God has a picture and he's painting this beautiful canvas of our lives," says Kelly. "Something that looked so dark and so evil can be made into this beautiful masterpiece. It still doesn't make sense, but I don't know that God would have gotten hold of my heart and unveiled some of the things in my heart if I still had my dad." Kelly now sees her relationship with God in a whole new light, and she understands that her father's death was the catalyst for her growth.

Kelly was now able to take the good news of Easter, which was the first holiday following her dad's death, and apply it to her situation. She realized that our hope has to be in the cross, because Christ died to make everything right. Jesus died for all our transgressions—for suicide, murder, adultery, lying, pride, and even sin that we are not aware of. It is finished – covered by the blood of the lamb. We are all redeemed if we choose Him, if we choose to trust Him no matter what. Kelly realized that God doesn't dish out favors based upon how good you've been or how much you do for Him. God offers His grace to all. His unconditional love countered that performance-based thinking Kelly had deeply held onto since childhood.

Grief, as most come to know, is a long and bumpy journey through hills and valleys. Kelly experienced difficulty in reading the Bible at times, and sometimes the mere task of opening the cover was a challenge. Many grievers have a feeling of having "done this before and being disappointed." Some are afraid to get close to God because they don't want Him to hurt them. But the goal is to put our trust in God and our hope in Him.

The summer following her dad's death, Kelly and her husband signed up for a mission trip to Brazil. Kelly second-guessed herself and her purpose for taking the trip, feeling inadequate. She wondered how she could give of herself when she felt she had nothing to give. How could she preach God's faithfulness to others when she was still struggling with it in her grief?

But we serve a mighty God capable of anything, and Kelly came back with amazing stories about her trip. She formed an immediate connection with a pastor in Brazil who openly shared his own personal, heartbreaking history of being suicidal. Kelly recalls crying uncontrollably at the lunch table during their conversation. So in the midst of her mission trip, where she had hoped to serve others, Kelly herself was the one who was ministered to. Kelly was blown away to learn that God had placed her in the presence of a group of people who could completely empathize with her and understand her loss; amazingly, every girl on the trip had lost their fathers early in life.

"It was totally due to God's hand that I had gone on the Brazil trip," says Kelly. "It was so providential. I realized that I'm not the only one in the world who lost a loved one. It just feels like that when you're going through it." God directed Kelly's eyes toward heaven and she began to realize God's promise of eternal life. It was as if He was saying, "My creation is perfect, but you live in a world that's full of sin. That's why I gave my Son, so that you might overcome your sin and have heaven and the perfection I created for you. I want you to have a longing for eternity and choose to give your life to me."

Two weeks after they returned from their trip, Kelly found out that she was pregnant. She wondered how she would manage, feeling so unsure of herself due to her grief. But God's faithfulness prevailed, and God showed Kelly His love for her through her new eyes as an expectant mother. She would soon learn the immense love a parent feels for a child, reflecting God's love for us.

"When I delivered Gaylen, she had dark hair and dark skin, and it was just like this picture of my dad," says Kelly. "I cried and thanked God for this precious gift, because every time I look at her I think about my dad, and now I see so much of Mark in her too. I came to realize that nobody comes into this world or leaves this world unless God says so. He's the author of life." Kelly began to deal with the fact that her dad had accomplished everything God wanted him to do here in this life. She understands God didn't cause the death, but allowed it to happen according to His will. And then, He gave her the most precious gift – a beautiful, healthy baby girl.

"Just having Gaylen is teaching me so much about who God is, who I am not, and how much I'm dependent upon Christ as a parent and as a person," says Kelly. "I'm still learning to let some barriers down, to let my heart open back up, and grow in my relationship with God. In everything, God indeed continues to be faithful."

> *"For God can use ALL things for the good of those who love Him and who are called to his purpose." (Romans 8:28, NIV 1984)*

Perspective
Rev. Haas

Perspective is an amazing thing. A story is told about John Wesley, the founder of the movement in England that became the Methodist church. It seems that Wesley was walking through the woods one day when suddenly a huge bear came upon him. He began to run like crazy, but he could tell the bear was gaining on him. So he threw himself down to the ground, clasped his hands together and began to pray loudly, "Oh Lord, save me from this terrible beast!" Whereupon the bear threw himself down on the ground, clasped his paws together and prayed loudly, "Oh Lord, I thank you for the bounty of this meal!" Same event, different perspective!

Perspective is defined as a "way of regarding situations or topics" according to Princeton University's WordNet.

Consider the story in the book of Luke about Peter's calling. As you read this, look for clues about Peter's perspective of himself versus Jesus' perspective of Peter.

> One day as Jesus was standing by the Lake of Gennesaret, with the people crowding around him and listening to the word of God, he saw at the water's edge two boats, left there by the fishermen, who were washing their nets. He got into one of the boats, the one belonging to Simon, and asked him to put out a little from shore. Then he sat down and taught the people from the boat. When he had finished speaking, he said to Simon, "Put out into deep water, and let down the nets for a catch." Simon answered, "Master,

we've worked hard all night and haven't caught anything. But because you say so, I will let down the nets." When they had done so, they caught such a large number of fish that their nets began to break. So they signaled their partners in the other boat to come and help them, and they came and filled both boats so full that they began to sink. When Simon Peter saw this, he fell at Jesus' knees and said, "Go away from me, Lord; I am a sinful man!" For he and all his companions were astonished at the catch of fish they had taken, and so were James and John, the sons of Zebedee, Simon's partners. Then Jesus said to Simon, "Don't be afraid; from now on you will catch men." So they pulled their boats up on shore left everything and followed him. (Luke 5:1-11, NIV 1984)

In this passage, Peter reacts very strongly to Jesus' call to follow him. We can imagine the scene, as he drops to his knees in humiliation before the Lord and says, "Go away!" He might have covered his face with his hands or looked off to the lake, avoiding eye contact with Jesus and wishing he could flee. He was awash in a sense of his own unworthiness, overwhelmed with his sin and his inadequacy to follow the Son of God, the Messiah.

Meanwhile, Jesus is experiencing the moment completely differently. He is looking upon a strong fisherman, a man of possibility, a man upon whom He knows He will build His church. Jesus doesn't see the sin; he sees the potential. He could have chosen any man in Israel to follow him, a rabbi, a temple leader, a scribe, a rich landowner; yet he chose Peter. And Jesus' perspective was the only one that mattered. Peter followed Jesus and became the rock upon whom the church was founded.

At the Guggenheim museum you can listen to tour guides in the different galleries explaining the paintings. Recently, one such guide led her group of tourists to an oil painting of what appeared to be a cocktail party scene. The men in the painting wore tuxedoes, and the women were dressed up in cocktail dresses and were quite bejeweled. A singer and a piano player could be seen in the background, confirming the perspective that it was a party scene. The guide said that the name of the painting is Paris Society, painted by Max Beckmann in 1931. So the name confirmed the perspective that this was a social gathering. Then she asked the group what they saw in the use of color, and people began to realize something was off in the picture. "The colors are vivid, with strong reds, yellows and oranges, but also somewhat gloomy," one woman responded. "There are a lot of gray and black tones amidst the bright tones" agreed another. The guide asked them what the feeling was at the party, and everyone realized that nobody in the painting looked like they were having any fun. Nobody was making eye contact or smiling...in fact there is a pervasive feeling of gloom that comes out of the party, thought many.

The guide then pointed out a person in the lower right hand corner of the painting and the group realized this man wasn't just gloomy; he looks as though he is in deep despair, as he is holding his head in his hands. On top of that, his color is such an ashen gray that he looks like death, suggested a man in the group. The guide confirmed the death pallor on the man and said that this character was actually the real German ambassador in 1931. "Why is he so distressed?" an observer asked. "Remember the title, year and name of the painter," replied the guide. She explained, "This is a picture of Paris Society in 1931, right on the eve of the Second World War and the overtaking of Europe by the Third Reich. And the painter is a German. That's why the German ambassador is in despair." Finally the guide instructed the group to find the other face in the painting wearing a death pallor.... and there he was, right in the center of the painting—Adolph Hitler himself. Everyone had missed him until that moment; because viewers didn't know where to look, he had just blended right in. The painter has depicted him wearing the death pallor he was already inflicting on Europe while Paris society partied, the guide explained.

"We know all this about the painting because Max Beckmann's widow gave this description of it after he died," the guide finished.

You see, the widow knew the painter... and knowing the painter and the painter's perspective is the only way to make sense of what you're seeing. Consider this; Jesus was the painter of Peter's life; He breathed life into him, brushstroke by brushstroke. He was present when Peter was formed in the womb; he looked deep into Peter's soul and knew the man that he was and was to become, and he chose Peter to follow Him.

Just as Jesus' perspective of Peter was more important than Peter's perspective of Peter, His perspective of your loss more important than yours. Jesus is the painter of the work that is your life, including this death that has sneaked in while you didn't know where to look.

Perspective is a critical aspect of how we process our grief, as it causes us to ask the question "How do I see my loss? What is my perspective on this death?" And when our perspective is "This death has ended my life" then the question becomes, can anything change my perspective so that I might survive this?

Where we start the process will determine where we end, and surely the nature of the loss defines our perspective in the beginning. While all losses are devastating and lead all mourners to a common place of emptiness and pain, some deaths are foretold while others catch us terribly and completely off guard. The loss of a 96-year-old grandparent who has been suffering with a terminal illness will feel different than the death of a six-year-old child who is killed in a car accident. This must be acknowledged. Each mourner's perspective is unique and personal, and no one can truly say, "I know how you feel."

Even members of the same family processing the same death will have different reactions as each one processes the loss in an individual way. Our perspective shapes our experience.

But more importantly, as we process our grief we should be asking ourselves, "What is God's perspective of death?" In the end, God, who paints life and death into being, brush stroke by brush stroke, has the only perspective that really matters.

Job struggled with perspective when God allowed Satan to test his righteousness. In a matter of days he lost everything, including his children, who perished together when a mighty wind from the desert caused their house to collapse on them. He was left with the company of useless friends for comfort. In the midst of his tremendous loss, he cries out that he cannot find God anywhere in the void of all that has been taken from him:

Then Job replied:

> "*Even today my complaint is bitter; his hand is heavy in spite of my groaning. If only I knew where to find Him; if only I could go to His dwelling! I would state my case before him and fill my mouth with arguments. I would find out what he would answer me, and consider what he would say to me. Would he vigorously oppose me? No, he would not press charges against me. There the upright can establish their innocence before him, and there I would be delivered forever from my judge. But if I go to the east, he is not there; if I go to the west, I do not find him. When he is at work in the north, I do not see him; when he turns to the south, I catch no glimpse of him.*" (*Job 23:1-9, NIV 1984*)

Part of Job's perspective about the loss of his property and the death of his sons and daughters was that God was nowhere to be found. Indeed, many people feel the exact same thing. Their perspective of death includes the notion that they have experienced the complete abandonment of God. Even Jesus, in His moment of agony on the cross, cried out:

> *"My God, my God! Why have you forsaken me?"* (Matthew 27:46, NIV 1984)

But God's response to Job illuminates exactly where God is and has been in the midst of all of our temporal struggles:

> *"Where were you when I laid the earth's foundation?*
> *Tell me, if you understand.*
> *Who marked off its dimensions? Surely you know!*
> *Who stretched a measuring line across it?*
> *On what were its footings set,*
> *or who laid its cornerstone*
> *while the morning stars sang together*
> *and all the angels shouted for joy?"* (Job 38:4-7, NIV 1984)

God reminds Job that as Author of creation of the earth, He was there when the morning stars sang their first song together; He was the One who marked off the depth and breadth of the earth. He was and always will be THERE…. and where was Job? In this seemingly harsh response, God is reminding Job about the temporary nature of his fleeting life in comparison to the magnitude of creation, which has been brought forth over the span of eternity. In God's perspective, Job's complaint is but a fleeting second in the context of Time. And God is in every moment of our being.

From God's perspective, death is not the worst thing. In fact, death isn't even the last thing; death never gets the last word. Hear these words from the book of Romans:

"Who shall separate us from the love of Christ? Shall trouble or hardship or persecution or famine or nakedness or danger or sword? No, in all these things we are more than conquerors through him who loved us. For I am convinced that neither death nor life, neither angels nor demons, neither the present nor the future, nor any powers, neither height nor depth, nor anything else in all creation, will be able to separate us from the love of God that is in Christ Jesus our Lord." (Romans 8:35-39, NIV 1984)

So we see here that death cannot separate us from God. Hear these words now from Revelation 21:

And I heard a loud voice from the throne saying, "Look! God's dwelling place is now among the people, and he will dwell with them. They will be his people, and God himself will be with them and be their God. He will wipe every tear from their eyes. There will be no more death or mourning or crying or pain, for the old order of things has passed away." He who was seated on the throne said, "I am making everything new!" Then he said, "Write this down, for these words are trustworthy and true." He said to me: "It is done. I am the Alpha and the Omega, the Beginning and the End. To the thirsty I will give water without cost from the spring of the water of life." (Revelation 21:3-6, NIV 1984)

God's perspective of death is that death is not the end. It is not final, nor is it forever. God's perspective is that by the power of the resurrection there is a death of death, as believers receive eternal life upon their death. Thus death is a short transition, a passing over from life to Life.

"For God so loved the world that he gave his one and only Son, that whoever believes in him shall not perish but have eternal life." (John 3:16, NIV 1984)

"Very truly I tell you, whoever hears my word and believes him who sent me has eternal life and will not be judged but has crossed over from death to life. Very truly I tell you, a time is coming and has now come when the dead will hear the voice of the Son of God and those who hear will live." (John 5:24-25, NIV 1984)

Paul's words in 1 Corinthians 15 give great clarity to the non-permanence of death, explaining that our current bodies, which are perishable here on earth, will put on the imperishability of eternal life. At that time we are given immortality, a life everlasting through the resurrection of Jesus:

I declare to you, brothers and sisters, that flesh and blood cannot inherit the kingdom of God, nor does the perishable inherit the imperishable. Listen, I tell you a mystery: We will not all sleep, but we will all be changed— in a flash, in the twinkling of an eye, at the last trumpet. For the trumpet will sound, the dead will be raised imperishable, and we will be changed. For the perishable must clothe itself with the imperishable, and the mortal with immortality. When the perishable has been clothed with the imperishable, and the mortal with immortality, then the saying that is written will come true: "Death has been swallowed up in victory. Where, O death, is your victory? Where, O death, is your sting?" (I Corinthians 15:50-55, NIV 1984)

So what can it mean for mourners to take on God's perspective of death and loss?

It means that this time of separation is only temporary. While the rest of your life will be spent without the one you love, the rest of your life is but a blink of an eye in the scope of eternity. Just as those highly anticipated moments in our lives seem forever to get here, like kids who wait for Christmas or brides who wait for their wedding day, those events are but a blink of an eye in the scope of an eternal lifetime. If you've been married for a while, think back. Do you remember how fleeting your wedding was? How quickly it went, after all the months of preparation? If you have adult children, think back about their toddler and elementary years. How often do we say, "I can't believe how fast it went"? If you've graduated from college, think about how quickly those four years flew by, in hindsight.

The problem with grieving is that it slooowwws down time. We become suspended in an artificial reality that is all too real. Days are long and nights are longer because we are stuck in the moment of our crisis like a fly caught in tree sap. Our movements and our thoughts are sluggish. It takes forever to get simple things done, to make sentences come together, to remember why we have walked into a particular room. It is not uncommon to forget even names of friends and acquaintances after the shock of a death. Grief can make us feel as though we are swimming in tar, trying to reach a distant shore that keeps moving farther away and the swim is taking forever. Embracing God's perspective that death and mourning are only temporary states can begin to help us shake off our sluggishness and get on with what is the rest of our short existence here. Hear these words of Psalm 90 that offer us a perspective of how God measures time:

> *A thousand years in your sight are like a day that has just gone by, or like a watch in the night.* (Psalm 90:4, NIV 1984)

In God's perspective of time, a thousand years are like a day; so the eighty or so years of our lifetime are just a blink of an eye in the scope of our real life span, our eternal and everlasting life.

It means that death isn't the end. What joy can fill our hearts to know that! If we take on God's perspective that death isn't final, then we can begin to process our loss as more of a kind of misplacement. Sometimes in life, we lose things that we know will never be found again. When you lose one earring from your favorite pair, you can look for months and know you will never find it again; it is gone forever. But other times we simply misplace things, like car keys and sunglasses, for example. We are sure they are somewhere in the house, in a purse, or in a pocket, but we have to look in a couple of places before we find them. Understanding death from God's perspective is more like that; our loved one is not lost forever, just in another place, waiting to be reclaimed when we die and join them in eternity. That means we don't have to give in to the terrifying fear that comes with a true loss. Our loved ones are never truly lost from us; they are simply misplaced from this life because they are placed into another life, and we are guaranteed to find them again at the time of our own passing.

And comfort comes from knowing that they are never, ever misplaced from God, for He is in life, in death, and in eternity. That's what He was trying to tell Job. Paul explains this well in I Corinthians 15:

> *But Christ has indeed been raised from the dead, the firstfruits of those who have fallen asleep. For since death came through a man, the resurrection of the dead comes also through a man. For as in Adam all die, so in Christ all will be made alive. But each in turn: Christ, the firstfruits; then, when he comes, those who belong to him. Then the end will come, when he hands over the kingdom to God the Father after he has destroyed all dominion, authority and power. For he must reign until he has put all his enemies under his feet. The last enemy to be destroyed is death.*
> (1 Corinthians 15:20-26, NIV 1984)

And it means that death does not render us alone. Even though we feel alone, abandoned and forsaken, there is never a moment when the God who was present before time is not present in our anguish. Even Jesus felt abandoned, but he was not, as He experienced the power of resurrection and was reunited with the Father. Sin is the only thing that can ever separate us from the Father, but death never can, and so we can find comfort in knowing that in the depth of our loneliness, God is near.

Jesus came in the flesh to embody the love of the Father for the world. He is the incarnate Lord, the walking-divine who instructs us about the intentions and perspectives of our eternal God. He experienced earthly life, earthly death and heavenly resurrection. He appeared to His disciples just before his final ascension into heaven. Hear what Jesus had to say about abandonment:

> *Then Jesus came to them and said, "All authority in heaven and on earth has been given to me. Therefore go and make disciples of all nations, baptizing them in the name of the Father and of the Son and of the Holy Spirit, and teaching them to obey everything I have commanded you. And surely I am with you always, to the very end of the age." (Matthew 28:18-20, NIV 1984)*

"And surely I am with you always." This is Jesus' reminder to you today that He is with you in your grief walk. He will never abandon or forsake you. There is no deep, dark place of sorrow that you can go without Him. There is no place of anger that He cannot withstand with you; there is no place of hopelessness that He will not traverse by your side; there is no place of loneliness that he does not occupy.

You are not alone.

Thanks be to God.

And so knowing that you are not alone, knowing that your time of separation is but a brief flicker on the timeline of your life, and knowing that your loved one has only been misplaced for a moment and is waiting to be found by you when you die, it is time to move forward into a new perspective.

Fashion your new perspective after the Painter, who sees death as a doorway to Life. Fashion your new perspective after the Resurrected One, who went before us in that journey. Fashion your new perspective as a mourner who never walks alone in the valley of the shadow of death; for what is a shadow, if not a brief passing of a cloud before the sun? Death is nothing more than a shadow! Fashion your new perspective after the One who set the stars and planets in the sky and who created time. In time, your grief will pass into a new perspective that you can live with. For you were meant to live and have life abundant. It's just a matter of perspective.

CHAPTER FOUR

Sherry

They say the best things in life are free, and for Sherry Davidson, that gift came at an unexpected time in an unexpected place. Sherry grew up in Alabama with her mom (Jeanne), dad (Fred), and sister (Susan). They were a close family who did many things together. One exception was going to church on Sundays. The family united became the family divided on Sunday mornings, with Fred and Susan attending church regularly and Jeanne and Sherry staying at home many Sundays. Sherry and her mom did attend church some, because "it was the right thing to do to go to church," Sherry said, but while her sister, Susan, embraced church, Sherry hated it.

As a child, Sherry's mother attended church with the family who adopted her at age ten, and then again during her married life up until Sherry was born. But Jeanne was never very active in her church. Sherry battled with pneumonia as a baby, prompting her mother to remain at home many Sundays with her, which may explain how Jeanne fell into a pattern of missing church. As Sherry got older, she decided for herself that she was not interested in going to church and stayed home on Sundays. Jeanne felt it was okay to be a person of faith and not be in worship on Sunday; however, she did attend church for Christmas, Easter, baptisms, and weddings.

Jeanne Robertson was considered a true Southern Belle growing up, very "magnolia", very proper. For this reason, she never really talked about certain topics she felt were private. One was her life before adoption and the other was her faith. "Mother *never* discussed her faith," Susan said. "Daddy called her a deep thinker, but she didn't talk about her faith."

When Fred fell ill with Alzheimer's and dementia, Jeanne became the sole caregiver for nine long years. Since Fred had dedicated his life to the church, Jeanne expected the church family and pastoral staff to reach out and support him through his illness like churches do. But, to her dismay and disappointment, the support she expected was not forthcoming, and Jeanne felt very hurt by what she felt was a lack of concern. Her husband had given his life in Christian service, and so Jeanne struggled with bitterness toward the church for ignoring her husband when he needed them the most. "Mother wanted to see the love from the church people," Sherry said.

Following her husband's death in 1997, Jeanne replaced care-giving by doing the things she loved most, like playing bridge, being with friends, and spending time with her grandkids, but her daughters said she never felt physically well. *The stress from daddy being very sick caused mother's health to deteriorate*, they concluded. She developed shingles in 2002 with lingering pain that was a large part of her just not feeling up to par.

Widowed and living alone, Jeanne was forced to call 911 for herself in January 2005 during an episode of illness. Doctors prescribed her medicine and attempted to send her home, but Jeanne knew her own body better and realized something was wrong. As the hospital tried to release her, a physician friend coaxed the staff into letting her stay when her blood pressure dropped and could not be stabilized. Three hours later she landed in emergency surgery followed by a stay in ICU. Jeanne had a ruptured sphincter muscle, wasn't eating, and was losing weight. Once home, Susan stayed with her mom a good bit to watch over her, taking turns with Sherry. Jeanne continued to lose weight and was in and out of the hospital, assisted living facilities, and nursing homes in Montgomery, Alabama.

The family's hope and desire was that Jeanne would recover and be able to live on her own in a senior housing situation. First though, she would have to regain her strength, either through a temporary stay at an assisted living facility or by living with one of her daughters. Susan woke up one morning in August 2005 with a strong feeling that she needed to call Amber Forest, a local assisted living facility in Georgia where she lived. They had two rooms available, forcing Susan to make a quick decision. She wanted to consult with her sister, but Sherry was in Jamaica with her husband celebrating their 25th wedding anniversary. Susan knew it would be impossible to get in touch with her. Call it a coincidence—or a God-incidence—but Susan's phone rang at that very same time, and it was Sherry. Susan was elated that Sherry would call from Jamaica just at the time she needed to consult with her regarding this latest development.

However, Susan would soon discover that Sherry was not in Jamaica, but rather in Huntersville, North Carolina at a local emergency room. Her week-long anniversary celebration was cut short when Sherry's husband, James began experiencing serious heart problems. Forced to fly home because of this emergency, Sherry was now accessible and available to help Susan make a decision about Amber Forest. Sherry calls it *God-timing.*

They all agreed Amber Forest would be an excellent temporary living facility, but Jeanne only agreed to tolerate a one-month stay. In the meantime, Jeanne's house sold in Alabama (more God-timing), prompting her to modify her one-month agreement and remain there three months. The sisters were elated with her decision. Jeanne wasn't very happy about the move, but an event yet to come would change her entire perspective. "We absolutely loved it. The people there were so great. Mother wanted to hear this one song, *The Cha Cha Stomp (Charlie Brown)*. It's a good dancing song that goes left-foot-stomp, right-foot-stomp, cha -cha. And she also liked the Electric Slide," said Sherry. "The staff there was so nice, and played the song for her when she asked. We were also able to paint mother's room and make it real cute. Just temporary you know."

Jeanne's weight loss persisted, and doctor's felt it necessary to assist her nutrition through the insertion of a bolus feeding tube. Sherry remembers the day with perfect clarity. *Coming back in the car from the hospital, there was a part where she was swollen with this tube sticking out of her pants, and mother was so funny saying "look I have a winkie." She had a sense of humor. Her personality was hilarious until the day she died.*

Jeanne was doing well, but had quit eating. Family speculated the decreased appetite issue was either a result of the drugs Jeanne had been prescribed or a possible stroke, but they would later discover she suffered from a condition called anorexia. She had already been diagnosed with Helicobacter Pylori and tested for Clostridium Difficile. Jeanne despised the feeding tube, but nurses were successful in getting some much-needed nutrition in her through it. "Its funny how mother talked about food, watched the Food Network on television, was obsessed with food, but would not eat," Sherry said.

In November 2005, approximately three months following Jeanne's arrival at Amber Forest, Sherry traveled from her home in North Carolina to spend Thanksgiving with her mom. When she walked into her mother's room and saw her current condition, Sherry sensed she was dying and chose to remain in Georgia indefinitely. Jeanne's room at Amber Forest became Susan and Sherry's hangout. With a computer in her room, Jeanne's daughters were able to maintain their personal work obligations and still be with their mom. With time on her hands, Sherry even volunteered at Amber Forest helping them develop forms in their computer system that they still use today. Sherry and Susan even became friends with the "house cat" known to roam the halls of Amber Forest in search of a little handout. The sisters were pushovers for the cat and left their mother's door ajar, allowing the cat to freely come and go, always making sure to save some leftover chicken for kitty.

With her physical care being well managed by the wonderful Amber Forest staff and Hospice, family members focused their attention on Jeanne's spiritual care. Susan's husband, Robert, was working a weekend-long spiritual church retreat called the Walk to Emmaus. Robert had the opportunity to seek advice there from two Christian pastors during a special chapel time. He asked them, "How do I talk to my mother-in-law, an intensely private woman, about her faith?" Their response, "Just ask her." So, upon his return, with that intention, Robert went to Amber Forest to see Jeanne. Susan let Robert go by himself that morning, but quietly prayed at home for Robert's meeting with mother. Although very out of character for Robert, he sat down by his mother-in-law's bedside, cut to the chase and said, "Jeanne, do you believe in Jesus?" and she replied, "Of course, don't you?" Thirty minutes after Robert had left the house, all of a sudden Susan said she felt an overwhelming need to move from an attitude of prayer to one of thanksgiving and praise for God, which coincided with the time Robert had received mother's confirmation of faith. God is good! It couldn't have been any easier, but the fear many of us have initiating those types of conversations about faith, especially with private people, can often render us mute. When asked how Robert felt after his visit, his wife replied, "Robert came home ecstatic. There was a definite change in mother when Robert went by there."

Sherry recalls one day when she was going to the store and asked mother if she was going to be there upon her return. Mother just looked at Sherry and said, "I'm just waiting on *Him* to take me you know. I'm gonna be here." Sherry just loved her mother's personality. One time when the pastor from Susan's local church came by to visit, Jeanne greeted him with, "Chuck, well you're just the best looking thing I've ever seen."

Spending time with their mom during those last few weeks was one of the greatest blessings for Sherry and Susan, but what transpired in the last few days of Jeanne's life was eternally life changing for Sherry. Over the course of several days, as Jeanne was deteriorating rapidly toward death, she would look up with eyes wide open and experience glimpses of Heaven. Inhaling with a deep cleansing breath, one day she said, "Oh my! Nobody told me— (big sigh), it's beautiful, the flowers (big sigh) —oh they're magnificent!" Then she would talk about the music, the love and would recount, *I've never experienced anything like this before!* Sherry and Susan were her captive audience just sitting there in wide-eyed amazement.

The experiences of Heaven continued during a fifteen-day process where at different an unexpected times Jeanne would see the awe-inspiring beauty of Heaven. Repeatedly, she described Heaven using adjectives like bright, shiny, beautiful, and filled with color! There was one day when Jeanne lifted up her arms toward the sky and cried out, "Daddy, oh I've missed you so! Mother, my mother." She would try to impart her new wisdom to her daughters as best she could. *They live and they die.* "Everything mother saw just made me feel much more comfortable. I know that," said Sherry. Susan remembers another day when mother's encounter with Heaven led her to exclaim, "The flowers! The music! The love! Nobody told me (big sigh), the Greek columns (big sigh)! The colors, they're b-e-a-u-t-i-f-u-l, oh they're singing." Then Jeanne would clap her hands to different parts of the room. Susan said that one time her mother pointed her index finger saying, "I'm not going until I see it all," and then folded her arms, put them under the covers, and closed her eyes in stout rebellion.

Jeanne's experience led her to grab hold of anyone who would come into her room or wander down the quiet halls of Amber Forest, in hopes of sharing her faith with passion and child-like wonder. She needed everyone to understand how amazing Heaven was! It could be the hospice nurse, the nurse's aide, the doctor, or the kitchen staff, but Jeanne did not care. All were fair game in Jeanne's plan to share the gospel. "Mother had a greater spiritual awareness in the last three weeks of her life, in my opinion, than she ever had before," Susan said. "She was very free to share it with anyone who came into the room about how beautiful every person was, and she wanted everyone to know about *the love, the love.*"

This was the private Southern Belle who didn't talk about her faith or actively attend church. This was the woman who stayed home on Sundays. But something had changed. Jeanne had experienced an encounter with the Living God like never before, and it was amazing! She had the opportunity to impact lives for Christ, and knowing her time on Earth was limited, she seized every one of those opportunities with vigor and determination. But, the most significant life she changed through her witness and testimony those last few days was that of her daughter, Sherry. Jeanne vehemently made her daughter promise to start attending a church and learn all she could about a relationship with God, and Sherry replied, "I don't know what you're talking about, but I'm going find out and I will start going to church."

As much as the family enjoyed this new spiritually open side of Jeanne, the time came when she would decline further, having the desire to neither eat nor drink, but instead could only take water sprayed in her mouth. Jeanne didn't want the water to drink. Her request was that it be sprayed on her for comfort. The grandchildren for years had used an old nickname for Jeanne which was "Nunnie," so when Jeanne started asking for the water spray they created a new nickname—"Hydroponic Nunnie," which has provided a memory to treasure with laughter.

Knowing the end was very near, Sherry summoned her husband Joe, to come to Georgia as they prepared to say goodbye. Jeanne was not talking at this point, but the family was confident she could still hear them. "Joe, just talk to her," Sherry said. "Even if you think she can't hear you, just talk to her." Not knowing what to say, Joe started by singing the words, "Jesus Loves Me This I Know," and to their utter shock and amazement, Jeanne burst forth from her world of silence to continue the stanza with "Yes, I know, for the Bible tells me so." Sherry recollects, "We all about dropped. That was another shocker."

On November 22, 2005, two days before Thanksgiving, the girls left Amber Forest late and returned to Susan's house for some much-needed sleep. As Sherry steered the car into the driveway, she heard an unfamiliar song whose lyrics brought her to tears. It was called "Christmas Shoes" sung by Billy Goodwin of New Song with lyrics "It's Christmas Eve and these shoes are just her size…..And I want her to look beautiful—if mama meets Jesus tonight…." She felt as if the song was written just for her. They knew mother's time to go home with the Lord was very near, and the song just resonated in Sherry's heart about her feelings toward her own mother's imminent meeting with Jesus. Little did Sherry know, down the road, the significance this song would have in another chance encounter.

Sherry eagerly woke up the next morning and sprang out the door, hoping to be of some help in setting up Amber Forest's annual

Thanksgiving feast. She was excited about the special day with aromas of fresh turkey, sweet potatoes, and pumpkin pie permeating the halls. Upon her arrival at Amber Forest, Sherry's first order of business, though, was to check in on Mother, and to her dismay she discovered her mother lying in bed experiencing much-labored breathing. The nurses, familiar with the signs of impending death, began to prepare Sherry and to assist Jeanne in the final transition. Jeanne's hospice nurse, whom she endearingly had nicknamed "the old goat," knew Jeanne liked songs and reminded her of "Swing Low Sweet Chariot." The nurse told her, "Miss Jeanne, now when you see the chariot swing low you hop on and go" for she knew from experience that dying people often need permission to pass in order to let go.

Sherry was puzzled though, watching her mother flail her arms back and forth seemingly agitated yet unable to speak. "I didn't know what she was doing," Sherry said. "I called Susan and told her to get here now—something is different." They would later discover from the night nurse that the house cat had wrapped itself around Jeanne's neck to comfort her the night before, which explains why she was waiving her arms around—trying to tell Sherry about the cat incident. "I've laughed about that," says Sherry. "The cat snuck in there to give her comfort. I think the cat knew."

Susan arrived shortly after Sherry summoned her and began to read Jeanne a devotional called "Into Thy Hands", where family members place loved ones in God's hands for safe keeping, In that moment they all felt surrounded by God's love. "Then we prayed, and it got very quiet," Susan said. "Sherry was on the computer and I was holding mother's hand. I don't sing or hum normally, but I started humming "swing low, sweet chariot" and at that moment (10:23am on November 23rd, the day before Thanksgiving 2005) mother went home to be with the Lord." The day was filled with making decisions and preparations, but later that night after the families left, the Activities Director found the music to Mother's favorite songs. They went out in the lobby of Amber Forest, along with five or six of the aides, and Susan watched with laughter as they all danced the *Electric Slide and Cha Cha Stomp* in honor of mother.

When you talk to Sherry today you can sense that her new faith was her source of strength during the difficult journey of grief. Sherry says her faith played a role in her grief recovery "big time." She states, "I think my faith is stronger. I promised my mother I'd start going to a church and I did—I have. She gave me that little kick to continue the journey. My husband and I are now going to a Presbyterian church in South Carolina. Some friends in our neighborhood had asked us to come to their church, and I guess we needed a little encouragement. Now we sit in the front row and help with the offering. We are the ones inviting people to come! I think mother gave me faith in myself, and I'm not scared of a lot of things anymore. I used to be scared of things like driving by myself, of dying, but none of that matters anymore. I drive by myself and love it now. There's nothing I fear anymore. Its amazing—like amazing grace!" Faith was the good that came out of losing her mom—a priceless gift passed down like a family heirloom.

What an amazing transformation for Sherry's spiritual life. In addition, Sherry's husband, Joe, has also been changed through this experience. He has been attending church regularly and has recently completed the training to become a Mason (Freemason), a fraternal group of men committed to the concepts and ideals of brotherly love, charity for others and the search for truth whose activities focus on making the world a better place. Joe is even organizing a golf tournament to raise money in support of their charitable causes.

As Susan reflects on this experience with her mother she explains, "It was a process of the faith journey that continues, but the baton keeps getting passed. You're still walking the faith journey even though you're going through a very tough time of family illness, and through the process you continue passing on the faith." Susan also felt God showed Himself miraculously to her in lots of little things that people did throughout Jeanne's illness. Difficult situations worked out perfectly and with impeccable timing, like the time Sherry abruptly came home from Jamaica just when Susan needed her to help make important decisions.

Susan challenges others on the grief journey to look for the God things—those instances where God is at work regarding your job, when you get an appointment just when you need one, you receive a phone call at the moment you are thinking of the caller, or a card arrives in the mail just when you needed it. Susan also shared how often in grief it is difficult to pray, read, or study the Bible, but says not to be afraid to ask others to do that for you. "Getting your name on a church prayer list is so important," she said. "I don't know if we can convey the story of how truly sick mother was and what a miracle for a woman who never shared her faith story EVER to share it with every person who walked into the room in the last three weeks of her life. The people who were working at Amber Forest—it changed their lives. Every shift different people would come into the room to see how mother was doing. She would share her vision of heaven with everyone."

Sherry has used her experience of loss to connect with other grievers about her journey. One day, while delivering an order of t-shirts from her design print company to a customer at a local middle school, Sherry discovered that her customer, Lauren, had also lost her mother around the same time. They were organizing heaping piles of shirts as Sherry began to share the *Christmas Shoes* song and how much it meant around the time of her mother's death. Tears were streaming down both of their cheeks when they were suddenly joined by a PTA volunteer who graciously offered her services to help sort the mounds of t-shirts. Of course, Sherry and Lauren felt compelled to explain the nature of their sobbing, and what this volunteer said next was something Sherry could never have imagined. "The singer of the *Christmas Shoes* song is my Uncle Bill," said Wanda, subsequently bringing all three of them to tears.

Several months later, Sherry had another shirt order to deliver to the school, when she received a message that a school parent had left a gift in the office for Sherry to pick up. Sherry had no idea what it could be, but approached Lauren to find out. Lauren kept Sherry in suspense by prefacing the delivery of the gift with this question, "Do you remember our conversation in the parking lot months ago about the song?" Then, Lauren handed Sherry a picture, signed and autographed by all the members of the band New Song with an inscription that read—*Sherry, God bless you! PS Psalm 40:1-3.* Wanda had called in a favor from her Uncle Bill to provide that gift for Sherry who dearly loved his song. It was a very special moment for Sherry filled with more tears. Later that afternoon, Sherry was at home tidying up her kitchen when she heard a small crash in her bathroom. When she went to investigate, she discovered that one of the three heavy brass butterflies she displays on the side of her bathtub had fallen off onto the tile floor. It was the middle butterfly, and it was not something easily tipped over because of its weight. "Mother was with me. It was an "oh my gosh" day!" said Sherry.

Even with her newly found faith, Sherry knows the grief journey will not be an easy one. "I'm still having a hard time," she says. "How long does this take to get over? I talk about her all the time. There are so many things I don't want to let go of because they belonged to mother.

I found some gloves on the other day, and I remembered they were Mother's because I could smell her."

Sherry will dearly treasure all the things of her mother's that she has in her possession like those gloves, but she will treasure most the intangible gift of her mother's faith and experiences of Heaven which have completely and forever changed her life—eternally. They say the best things in life are free, and for Sherry Davidson, that gift came at an unexpected time in an unexpected place.

> *"I waited patiently for the LORD; he turned to me and heard my cry. He lifted me out of the slimy pit, out of the mud and mire; he set my feet on a rock and gave me a firm place to stand. He put a new song in my mouth, a hymn of praise to our God. Many will see and fear the LORD and put their trust in him." (Psalm 40:1-3, NIV 1984)*

Epiphany
Rev. Haas

The large, milky white whale known as the Beluga Whale has an interesting way of navigating their surroundings. Belugas were created with the power of "echolocation." Echolocation is the way Belugas find their way around in dark waters; basically it is a system where they send out a sound and then listen for the sound to echo off a solid object and return to them. They have a fascinating physiology that allows them to produce directional clicks in their nasal sacs in rapid sequences called trains. The click train passes through something called a melon located in their snouts, which acts like an acoustical lens to focus these sound waves into a beam, which is projected forward into the water in front of the whale. These sound waves travel at a speed of one mile per second, which is about four and a half times faster than sound waves travel through air. The sound waves bounce off objects in the water and return to the beluga in the form of an echo. The major areas of sound reception in the beluga are the fat-filled cavities of the lower jawbones. Then the sound travels to the middle ear, then the inner ear to the hearing centers in the brain via the auditory nerve. The brain then maps the information, and the whale knows exactly where he is.

Wouldn't it be amazing to have the power of echolocation? Especially in times of grief, the ability to find your way through the darkness of sorrow would be a blessing. One of grief's most predominant features is a feeling of disorientation. Days, time, conversations and events all seem to blur into one hazy never-ending moment. Climbing your way out of the fog of disorientation takes perseverance and help. If only there was a beam of light to show the way, something you could follow that would lead you through the black tunnel of hurt to the daylight of normalcy!

In the 2nd Chapter of Matthew we hear the familiar story of a beam of light that came to lead three men through the dark:

> Herod then arranged a secret meeting with the scholars from the East. Pretending to be as devout as they were, he got them to tell him exactly when the birth-announcement star appeared. Then he told them the prophecy about Bethlehem, and said, "Go find this child. Leave no stone unturned. As soon as you find him, send word and I'll join you at once in your worship." Instructed by the king, they set off. Then the star appeared again, the same star they had seen in the eastern skies. It led them on until it hovered over the place of the child. They could hardly contain themselves: They were in the right place! They had arrived at the right time! (Matthew 2:7-10, The Message)

"It led them on....and they could hardly contain themselves." The KJ version says they "rejoiced with exceeding great joy." It's easy to understand their ecstatic reaction; it's so good when you are in the dark and lost to finally find your direction, isn't it?

This chapter tells of the event we now call the Epiphany. In liturgical terms, Epiphany falls on January 6th and is celebrated on the Sunday closest to that day. It commemorates the revelation of the Christ child to the gentiles.

The word "epiphany" has an everyday meaning as well. When we hear someone say, "I finally had an epiphany about that," we understand that to mean that they have gained a new understanding on an issue. According to Dictionary.com, an epiphany is:

a sudden, intuitive perception of or insight into the reality
or essential meaning of something, usually initiated by some
simple, homely, or commonplace occurrence or experience.

This new intuitive perception acts like a bright star, shedding light on
the subject in a way we had never seen before.

Grief affords us the opportunity to have epiphanies about many
things. Along the way, it is not unusual to experience an epiphany
about the depth of the love and support of family and friends in a
way you never knew before. You might have an epiphany about your
own strength, or perhaps the lack thereof. Sad epiphanies about
loss, separation, and the finality of earthly life may come. But for all
believers, death can afford an epiphany about heaven, if only we look
for it. Like the three wise men, we need to seek it.

Early in my ministry I was interviewed by a troop of Girl Scouts, who
were studying different careers. They asked me what my favorite part
of my job is, and were stunned at my reply. "Ministry with the dying."
I answered. The girls squirmed and asked why. "Because," I told
them, "Being with someone when they die is one of the most sacred
moments I've ever experienced. It's when heaven opens up and you get
a glimpse. God is more present in that moment than any other."

The passing of your loved one has brought you to that moment.
Heaven has opened up, affording you a glimpse. What will you see,
if you look up?

The Bible has much to teach us about the nature of heaven. Jesus
describes it as a home with many rooms in John 14:

> *"Do not let your hearts be troubled. You believe in God; believe*
> *also in me. My Father's house has many rooms; if that were not*
> *so, would I have told you that I am going there to prepare a place*

for you? And if I go and prepare a place for you, I will come back
and take you to be with me that you also may be where I am.
You know the way to the place where I am going." (John 14:1-4,
NIV 1984)

This beautiful passage tells us that heaven is a place. It is a prepared
place, made ready for our arrival. And it has room for all of us! It also
assures us that it is Jesus himself who takes us to that place, reminding
us that indeed, nobody dies alone. What comfort that brings!

One of the ways that Jesus has prepared this home for us in heaven is
by creating a desire for it in our hearts on earth. As children of God
we all experience to some degree that internal tug of war between a
love for our earthly home and a longing for our heavenly home. We
experience this tug of war as an emptiness—a place of never quite
being satisfied with life. Too often we attempt to fill this hole in our
hearts with earthly substitutes, which can never work because God
has created this space to be filled only with Him.

C.S. Lewis writes, "Our lifelong nostalgia, our longing to be reunited
with something in other universe from which we now feel cut off,
to be on the inside of some door which we have always seen from
the outside...is the truest index of our real situation...we long to be
summoned inside, to be called home at last." (C.S. Lewis, <u>The Weight</u>
<u>of Glory</u> (San Francisco: Harper Collins, 1949) 41.)

The exiled Psalmist in Psalm 84 expresses his longing to be home
with God:

"How lovely is your dwelling place, O Lord of hosts!
My soul longs, indeed it faints for the courts of the Lord
My heart & my flesh sing for joy to the living God
Happy are those who live in your house, ever singing your praise!"
(Psalm 84:1-3, NRSV 1989)

Our spirit experiences the same longing to be reunited with our Father in Heaven, to be found by Him and to live finally in his eternal dwelling place. This longing is an ache that can't be satisfied by anything on earth because even the longing *itself* is of heaven. Joni Eareckson Tada, a paraplegic writer, expresses it this way:

"Your heart's home is in the heart of God. He has placed within you a yearning for himself, a desire to know him and understand what he is like. Every soul feels the void and the emptiness until it connects with the Master." (Joni Eareckson Tada, <u>Heaven: Real Home</u> (Grand Rapids: Zondervan, 1995)

All of our life we yearn for something more, and what we are yearning for is to go home to heaven. This is the preparation that Jesus refers to in John 14; not only is the place in heaven prepared for us, but we are prepared for the place when we accept Christ as our Savior. Our belief in Him guarantees our place in eternal life.

"For God so loved the world that he gave his one and only Son, that whoever believes in him shall not perish but have eternal life." (John 3:16, NIV 1984)

The Book of Revelation tells us this about heaven:

Then I saw "a new heaven and a new earth," for the first heaven and the first earth had passed away, and there was no longer any sea. I saw the Holy City, the new Jerusalem, coming down out of heaven from God, prepared as a bride beautifully dressed for her husband. And I heard a loud voice from the throne saying, "Look! God's dwelling place is now among the people, and he will dwell with them. They will be his people, and God himself will be with them and be their God. 'He will wipe every tear from their eyes. There will be no more death' or mourning or crying or pain, for the old order of things has passed away." He who was seated on the throne said, "I am making everything new!" Then he said, "Write this down, for these words are trustworthy and true." He said to me: "It is done. I am the Alpha and the Omega, the Beginning and the End. To the thirsty I will give water without cost from the spring of the water of life. (Revelation 21:1-6, NIV 1984)

And so from this we know the following:

1. Heaven is a place where we dwell with God, and He with us.
2. We never cry in heaven.
3. We do not die in heaven.
4. Nobody mourns in heaven.
5. Nobody feels any pain in heaven.
6. Everything will be new.

All too often at a funeral, people try to comfort us with throw-away lines like, "She is in a better place" and "Things happen for a reason" and "This is for the best." Of course when we hear those things, we sometimes just want to smack the person. Yet, in light of the epiphany that this scripture brings about regarding the true nature of heaven, these trite expressions actually come with a kernel of Biblical truth. Does this make you feel better? It should.

And often funeral sermons and homilies wax eloquently about the great feast in heaven that awaits us, where we will sit with the saints and eat from the heavenly banquets prepared by our Lord himself. We get the notion that there is great feasting in heaven from Isaiah 25:

> *On this mountain the LORD Almighty will prepare a feast*
> *of rich food for all peoples, a banquet of aged wine— the best*
> *of meats and the finest of wines. On this mountain he will*
> *destroy the shroud that enfolds all peoples, the sheet that covers*
> *all nations; He will swallow up death forever. The Sovereign*
> *LORD will wipe away the tears from all faces; he will remove*
> *his people's disgrace from all the earth. The LORD has spoken.*
> *(Isaiah 25:6-8, NIV 1984)*

None of us can truly begin to anticipate what heaven is like; but it will be no surprise to be embraced by our Lord, it will be no surprise to find ourselves in a place of no pain, no tears, no illness, and it will be no surprise to find ourselves at a love feast surrounded by angelic music and the pure worship of God, because that is what the scriptures tell us about heaven. But the rest remains a mystery.

Our entry into heaven begins a new chapter in our lives. Consider these lines from a song called *"Finally Home"* by Don Wyrtzen:

> Just think of stepping on shore and finding it Heaven,
> Of touching a hand and finding it God's
> Of breathing new air and finding it celestial,
> Of waking up in Glory and finding it home.

And so we come around to the beginning again, contemplating that star that was from heaven itself, and what it came to say to us. Realize that it still has something to say to you, especially in the dark place of your sadness.

Listen to how Robert Frost explains it in these beautiful words from his poem called "Choose Something Like a Star"

> O Star (the fairest one in sight),
> We grant your loftiness the right

To some obscurity of cloud –
It will not do to say of night,
Since dark is what brings out your light.
Some mystery becomes the proud.
But to be wholly taciturn
In your reserve is not allowed.
Say something to us we can learn
By heart and when alone repeat.
Say something! And it says, "I burn."

What the Epiphany star shining on your grieving soul says to you in this moment is, "I burn with an unquenchable fire of grace and mercy. I burn with the intensity hot enough to incinerate your deepest hurt. I burn with a love for you so bright it can forever drive the darkness away. I burn an everlasting burn and I will come to illuminate your world again. I am the star of Bethlehem, the Christ, the Messiah, the light of the world, a light no one, no depth of sadness nor height of despair can extinguish. I am Christ the Lord and I burn for YOU." And so how are you to respond to the Light of Heaven? Frost continues:

It asks a little of us here.
It asks of us a certain height,
So when at times the mob is swayed
To carry praise or blame too far,
We may choose something like a star
To stay our minds on and be staid.

(Robert Frost: The Road Not Taken: A Selection of Robert Frost's Poems (New York: Henry Holt and Company, 1916) 215-216.)

And so the only response we should make is to stay our minds on the star that represents heaven itself, and be staid. We should keep our eyes affixed toward the heaven that waits; to seek it, for that is where all believers live. Only by staying our minds on the Star of Bethlehem, Christ Jesus Himself, will we find true peace, healing and hope. Choose this epiphany for yourself today, and join with those wise ones who felt exceedingly great joy at knowing that Christ the Star burns for you. Heaven has opened up with this death you now mourn...what will you see, if you look up?

CHAPTER FIVE

Tom

It was an average day in an average month of an average spring in 2005 for Tom Barnes. Out of town on business, Tom and a co-worker were driving through Minneapolis rush hour to attend a group dinner meeting. Tom heard the familiar ring of his cell phone and answered to hear his wife's frantic voice on the other end. Little did Tom understand in that moment how much his entire life was about to change with her next words. In time, Tom would eventually come to realize that God planned for him to sit in the passenger seat of the rental car that day, because the news he was about to hear would devastate him. Eventually, they would destroy his marriage. That single phone call resulted in Tom's decision to move away from his family to a lonely apartment, alienated from friends and neighbors.

Tom grew up in Texas with his dad, mom, brother, and sister. His father was employed by NASA at the Johnson Space Center. He had a good childhood. He loved sports and enjoyed hanging out with his best friend, Michael Murphy. Tom spent a considerable amount of time over at Michael's house. While their families were similar in most respects, Tom's parents were not religious, but Michael's family was. Michael's dad was a Lutheran pastor, and the influence Michael's family had on Tom led him to begin attending church with the Murphy's when he was seven years old. Tom was even baptized, but says that looking back, he considered church with the Murphy's as a social outlet rather than a religious experience. As Tom and

Michael's friendship slowly faded away in high school, so did Tim's attendance in church.

Following high school, Tom set his sights on Texas A&M so that he might pursue his childhood aspiration to become a doctor. It had been Tom's desire since the age of six to help his pacemaker-dependant grandfather. Excelling in math and science, Tom modified his direction and ended up majoring in Biomedical Engineering, continuing on to obtain a master's degree in Industrial Engineering. Taking advantage of his father's connections, Tom often spent summers working for NASA. A company in Texas hired him one summer, shortly before finishing graduate school. To his surprise, Tom's new boss Sarah would later become his wife. His first day on the job happened to be Sarah's birthday, but her day was overshadowed by the breakup of a significant relationship. As time went on, Tom tried to support his new boss by offering to help her by doing things like maintaining the lawn at her house and other odd jobs, which led to the beginning of their relationship. They had a passion for softball, loved to travel (Sarah was an army brat), both possessed engineering degrees, and were close in age, which made spending time together seem effortless. "We were so much alike. We had fun," says Tom.

Tom completed graduate school in 1990 and gained employment with a pacemaker company in Freeport, Texas. Two years later in April 1992, Tom and Sarah knew they wanted to spend the rest of their lives together and made plans for their dream wedding. Life was great as they settled into their new life together as husband and wife. They were learning about one another and especially the art of "newlywed compromise". One of those compromises was their place of worship on Sunday mornings. Although he didn't embrace Catholicism, Tom agreed to attend Sarah's Catholic Church. "So we'd go to church, but I didn't get anything out of it," says Tom. "I was religious. I knew what I thought about God, but I didn't talk about it. I prayed by myself every night and that was perfect for me. I got a Bible in college and I read the whole thing—just to do it. It wasn't as if I read it and had a life-changing experience; I still prayed by myself at night."

Life moved along, and the first of their five children, Lauren, was born in 1994. Tom was enamored with his beautiful baby girl, and especially loved celebrating the first Christmas with Lauren in their life. Everything was perfect with the exception of one issue that began to arise between Tom and Sarah. It was the issue regarding Tom's disinterest in attending Sunday Mass. He began finding reasons not to go. "I'd put my head down and say my prayers," says Tom. "I was content with my life even though Sarah considered me not religious." Tom noticed his wife's unhappiness with his decision and felt pressured to join the church.

To escape tensions at home, Tom focused on his career. He received a promotion and through a work-related connection, pursued a job in Tokyo, taking over for a friend who was headed back to the United States. Tom and Sarah jumped at the opportunity for a Tokyo adventure – especially with the company absorbing all of the moving expenses. The position would not be a long-term position because of the expenses of keeping a foreign worker on the payroll, but it didn't sway their decision to go. Tom went ahead of the family, securing their new apartment, while Sarah remained behind to sell the family house.

Pregnant with their second child, Sarah flew to Tokyo in 1997 with Lauren. Not long after settling down in Tokyo, Tom and Sarah welcomed Caroline, baby girl number two, into their family, followed by their first son, John. Life seemed to be rolling right along. Tom and his family were happy and thriving on the lifestyle his amazing job afforded them in Tokyo.

The company policy even included paying for an annual return trip to the United States to see family. While visiting family in Virginia one summer, Sarah, four and a half months pregnant, went into premature labor, and the baby did not survive. Tom was not with them on this trip but immediately flew back to be with his wife and kids. Tom thought he was being supportive, but says that for some reason, Sarah was angry that he left Tokyo to come. "It was the beginning of the demise of our marriage," says Tom.

In 2002, the company informed them it was time to return to the US, but Sarah was pregnant again. They were allowed to postpone their move until the birth of Karen. Preparing to return to the US in 2003, Tom secured a sales position based in Georgia. He, Sarah and Lauren, went house hunting where they found their dream home equipped with the most perfect backyard pool and a spacious, dream kitchen that Tom says Sarah loved. The only thing it was missing was a wooden kid's play set with swings attached. Upon moving in, the list of to-do's seemed unending to Tom. He felt the pressure from his wife to get the play set built first and says, "We always knew that we needed to cover the pool, but it had steps and I didn't think it would be easy, and I never thought of a fence. I put chains on the back doors knowing the children could never reach that high. That was my protection."

One year later, Tom and Sarah were celebrating again as they welcomed child number five, Matthew, to the family. Although stepping back on United States soil put them back near family, and living in their new dream home was an added plus, Tom sensed Sarah longed for life back in Tokyo and the friends she left behind. In Tokyo, Tom says she had a social network; in the states she did not. "Raising five kids was tough," he says. "Then, add the pressure of an unhappy wife and my being gone on business much of the time. It is not surprising that we started to drift apart."

The kids were enrolled in the local elementary school and quickly made new friends. While playing at a friend's house one afternoon, Lauren was suspected by the mom of her playmate of stealing a small item. The mom initially remained silent about her suspicions, but confronted Sarah while out to lunch the following week.

Sarah knew it needed addressing, so one afternoon following a program at their church, Sarah arrived home with all the kids, and decided it was time for her talk with Lauren. With baby Matthew down for a nap, Sarah prepared a pizza to go into the oven while she let the other children head for the backyard play set – except Lauren. Caroline (7), John (4), and Karen (2 ½), were happily playing on the backyard swing, set giggling and enjoying themselves like all kids do. The older two must have been having so much fun that they did not notice that Karen had wandered away. The crystal blue swimming pool was nearby, remaining dangerously exposed without a cover or fence around it.

Minutes later, Caroline and John came inside, wondering if dinner was ready. Lauren was inside talking to Sarah, Matthew was asleep, and Caroline and John are there, but someone was missing – Karen! That's the moment that Sarah looked outside and saw Karen's little body lifelessly floating in the pool. The frantic call was made to 911, and Life Flight landed their helicopter in an empty residential lot across the street from their house. Neighbors rush out to see what is happening, and one quick-thinking neighbor immediately took the remaining children to her house next door to shield them from the heartbreaking scene.

Amidst the chaos, Sarah called Tom in Minneapolis to break the news. Tom recalls the brief phone call; *Panic-stricken, she told me Karen drowned, how she tried to save her, and it was believed Karen had a heartbeat before the helicopter took off. She was being taken to the closest Children's Hospital.*

"I was frantic as I called the travel agent – I had to get back that night," Tom recounts. "I didn't know if Karen was dead, alive, or in a coma. It was just a God thing that I wasn't driving the rental car, and that my good friend could handle getting me to the airport and on my way home. The second God thing was how during six o'clock rush-hour traffic in Minneapolis that I made it to the airport and was given a special emergency escort through security arriving at my gate with five seconds to spare."

Sitting on the plane with strangers surrounding him, Tim says he was not scared – that initially there was some indescribable peace. His mind began to wander, and the thought of Karen being brain dead rushed over him. He prayed to God, "*God this is in your hands. All right, God, if the next plane I see is going east toward home, then everything is okay, but if it's going west toward the sunset, then she's dead.*" I opened my eyes and saw a plane heading toward the sunset," says Tom. "I tried to prepare myself during the remainder of the flight. I was teary on the plane."

Tom's car was at the airport in Atlanta, but he had no idea how to navigate to the children's hospital. Prior to the flight taking off, Tom hurriedly left a voicemail for a co-worker, Mary, asking her to leave specific directions on his cell phone. It would be late when he arrived, and he was not in the best shape to be driving, but what other choice did he have? Little did Tom know that God would provide a driver for him. Mary had followed his flight information, and was patiently awaiting his arrival at the airport terminal. Tom attributes Mary's presence there as just another God thing.

Mary had also been in contact with the children's hospital staff all afternoon updating them on Tom's arrival. "They were keeping Karen in the bed until I could get there to hold her," says Tom. "I grabbed and hugged my wife as she kept saying she was sorry. I told her we would get through it – we were together. As I cried, I held Karen's cold, lifeless body for fifteen minutes." Not wanting to let go, Tom released his grip as the priest said a prayer, and in a daze Tom slowly left the room.

Tom returned to the airport to retrieve his car and drove home alone. It gave him time to think – to begin processing the reality of what felt like a dream sequence. His main concern was helping his wife. Sitting in their home office at 2 a.m., Tom and Sarah spent time talking, hugging, and crying. "It was a good conversation," Tom says. "When we went to bed, we were on the right track to get through this." With little sleep, they awoke in the morning to feel the pain and the shock setting in.

The neighbor brought the children back home around 9 a.m. the next morning. The children gathered on their parents' king-sized bed waiting for a family meeting to begin. Slowly and gently, they broke the grave news that the accident led to Karen's death. The children were 10, 7, 5, and Matthew was just an infant, so it was hard to know exactly how they would react to the news. Tom says they were all very quiet, and to this day, the girls prefer not to discuss the subject. The only child desiring to talk about Karen was John (age 5). John often would tell his dad, "If I could go back in time, I'd go back and save Karen."

Following the family meeting that morning, the whirlwind began. Out-of-town family arrived, neighbors stopped by, and the dreaded funeral arrangements had to be dealt with. Crying through it all, Tom says, they picked out the casket and the burial plot. Also on the to-do list was the eulogy that became another source of tension. During a late-night discussion with Sarah's family, Tom verbalized his fear the impact Karen's death would have on Sarah, because it happened on her watch. The family interpreted Tom's concern as blaming Sarah, and they were quick to inform her the next morning when she awoke. They were already under an extreme amount of stress, and family tension only magnified the situation like a lid on a pressure cooker.

With plans in place, the next event was the wake, which Tom says was surreal. "We each took a turn saying our goodbyes at the casket before anyone arrived," says Tom. "An older man I did not know came up to me and took me aside. He told me that he had also lost somebody special and challenged me to pick up the next penny I saw and read the inscription *In God We Trust*. He told me that it was Karen letting me know that she's watching out after me, and to trust God always. That had a huge impact on me. This unexpected encounter with a stranger pointed me back to my faith in God and reminded me to trust Him through the journey of grief."

Tom felt God was responsible for sending other signs to comfort him the following day, like the wild bunny (Karen's favorite) he saw out the window standing in the morning dew, the first blue rose of the season that appeared outside the kitchen window in their garden, or the perfect sunny day.

The funeral was a fitting tribute to a precious two-year-old little girl. "After the funeral, the neatest thing I remember was driving to the graveside and seeing policemen on every street corner saluting," says Tom. "It was very touching." A reception was held at the Country Club following the service. Adding to an already tense atmosphere, family members were concerned at the reception as they watched Tom accept an alcoholic drink.

"The day after the funeral, I could feel the tension between Sarah and me," says Tom. With friends gone and just family members left at the house, discussions, finger pointing, and accusations arose between them all—Sarah and her dad, Sarah and Tom, and Tom and his father-in-law. The result was an escalated, heated argument that resulted in Tom asking his in-laws to pack up and head back home. The gut-wrenching grief of tragically losing a precious toddler was bringing out the worst in them all. "When Sarah asked me why I kicked her father out of our house, we were divorced that second, we didn't have a chance," says Tom.

They pursued professional counseling to save their marriage and counseling for the children, but Tom knew the situation was hopeless when he was served with divorce papers that next summer. Tom agreed to move out in August 2006, and secured an apartment in town to be close to his children. "It was hard," Tom says. "Dealing with Karen's death and then losing my wife, my house, the daily interaction with my kids, and most of my friends who took sides in our divorce was a lot to take all at once. It was a risky time for me because I felt as if I didn't have a single friend, and I was living alone in a barren, cold place that was not my home." Bored with nothing else to do, Tom found himself drinking alcohol more regularly.

In December 2006, Tom returned home from a business trip to his lonely apartment around 1 a.m. With a cocktail in hand, he browsed through his mail, did some laundry, and checked e-mail. He finally went to bed at 4 a.m. only to arise at 8 a.m. – the time he was to pick up his children for his visitation. Without brushing his teeth or taking time for a shower, Tom quickly rushed out the door. Needing to pick up some personal belongings while he was there at the house, Tom headed up the staircase. Sarah got upset and called the police. Tom expressed indifference toward her and then proceeded to get the items he needed. He put the kids in the car, driving off before the police arrived. With red lights flashing, Tom was pulled over by local authorities with kids in tow. The police had been warned that Tom smelled of alcohol, so during the traffic stop he was asked to take a Breathalyzer test. Thinking he was fine, Tom nonchalantly consented to the roadside test. To his surprise, he was over the legal limit, handcuffed, and placed in the back of the patrol car all while his children watched in disbelief.

Authorities do not take the violation of DUI laws lightly as it places many lives in danger, but the seriousness of including children in the mix comes with a huge price tag – potentially one year in jail for every child in the car while driving under the influence. "By the grace of God the DUI was the best thing that could have happened to me," says Tom. "It was God's wake-up call. Part of the punishment is in the waiting though. I was arrested in December and had to wait six months until the court appearance. It would mean I'd lose my job while I was in prison."

During the six-month wait for his court appearance, Tom's company was bought out, and they were offering generous two-year pay severance packages for anyone willing to leave. Tom knew this was just what he needed. It would give him time off to grieve, and it would support his family while he was in prison. The one-year no compete clause in the severance agreement would not be hard to adhere to while sitting behind bars. "That was a thank-you God," says Tom.

As his court date finally arrived, Tom presented all his well-thought-out excuses for leniency and pleaded with the judge for understanding. The judge graciously sentenced him to one day in jail, revoking his driver's license for four months effective immediately. This meant he could not even drive home in his car conveniently parked in the courthouse parking lot. Tom says he approached a total stranger and humbly asked for a ride home. "We, the stranger and I, had a great conversation all the way back to my apartment," says Tom. Once home, he went into survival mode trying to figure out how to secure a temporary license needed for basic identification. His car is now stuck at the courthouse, the driver's license office is thirty minutes away, and he can no longer legally drive a motor vehicle.

With no mode of transportation to go anywhere, Tom decided to head to the apartment swimming pool and sit awhile to contemplate his next move. There he overheard two women whining and complaining about their own personal hardships. Tom chimed in to tell his story, winning the "my day beats your day" game. One of the women had no car due to a recent divorce, which financially bankrupted her, and so Tom proposed to let her drive his car if she would shuttle him where he needed to go. It was agreed, and for four months, Tom had himself a chauffeur and a new best friend. "That was another provision from God, finding Cheryl who could take me to get a temporary license," says Tom. "She is also very religious which is just what I needed at the time. It's incredible that our meeting happened when it did."

After serving his one-day sentence, Tom was uncertain about his future employment. He could not return to work at his old job, and he was legally not able to seek employment in the same field for a period of one year. So, Tom felt it was time to give back to the medical community that had been so good to him over the years. He sought out a volunteer position at the local hospital explaining to them his story of loss. Tom's desire was to reach out to others who had lost a child in a support/counseling role, but discovered certain credentials would be required for certification in those areas. In order for approval to visit with hospital patients and their families, Tom would have to successfully complete a fifty-hour class called Stephen Ministry. In the meantime, he volunteered driving the free hospital golf cart shuttle around the parking lot until his training was completed. For the next six months, Tom spent twenty hours a week driving people back and forth to their cars at the hospital helping them in any way he could. He would listen to their stories and offer to share his.

Tom had heard that getting into the Stephen Ministry class was sometimes hard to accomplish, so one day while volunteering at the hospital, he stopped by the Chaplain's office to enlist some support. "It was another God moment, because when I told the Chaplain my desire, he told me I was in luck. A new training class was starting that weekend at a local Methodist Church, and he would make the call to get me enrolled," says Tom. "The leaders of the class told me the first night we met that it would be the most amazing class I would ever take, and it truly was. It was incredible! I even began attending church there each Sunday, and the pastor there was awesome."

Enrolling in the class would present its challenges too. Tom would need help with his children on those nights when he had custody. Cheryl would once again be his angel. As a small token of appreciation for all Cheryl had done over the months while he attended class, Tom and his girls went shopping at a local Christian Bookstore to pick out a special gift. They chose a perfect little figurine with the inscription *Love, Peace, Joy* on the front, and presented it to Cheryl.

Through one of their many conversations, Tom confided in Cheryl about his desire to write a Christian book sharing his story of loss. Cheryl was brutally honest with Tom, telling him that he wasn't ready to write his story, because she felt he didn't know God and didn't understand the scriptures in the Bible. As a gift, Cheryl purchased a Bible for Tom and directed him to pour over it. She knew it was imperative for his spiritual growth, his relationship with God, and the subsequent other people he would minister to at the hospital to have a firm foundation.

Tom was uncertain where to begin because the last time he turned the pages of a Bible he was in college. He opened the Bible to 1 Timothy, and on the first page he turned to, Tom saw the phrase "love, peace, joy" – the same one found on the figurine the girls picked out for Cheryl. "That was incredible," says Tom. "Just when I started to open a Bible for the first time in years, the first thing I read is that phrase. That was cool."

Tom was beginning a new and exciting spiritual journey in his life and attributes the catalyst for change to the DUI and Karen's death." The Stephen Ministry training concluded the 50 hours of class with a graduation service at the host church. "During the ceremony, they give you a pin making it official," says Tom. "It was a big deal to me, and my parents and all my family had come to town for it as well." During his parents' visit, Tom's dad encouraged him to get a job in order to strengthen his position in the impending divorce. Tom knew his one-year of non-compete was almost up but hadn't been concerned about getting a job since he had two engineering degrees, an MBA, and international experience.

A plan was made to contact a recruiter ASAP, but before Tom could begin making those calls his phone rang with a very unexpected job offer from an old friend in Atlanta. "Another God thing," says Tom. "He was offering me a position as a technical field engineer that would put me in Atlanta near my kids – exactly what I wanted." From March 2008 until this call nine months later, Tom had essentially been volunteering at the hospital and wasting the rest of his time. This was the perfect job for him while going through the divorce. Tom could work out of his home, handle any scheduled court appearances or counseling appointments, and always be in town for scheduled visits with his kids.

Even with his new job in place, Tom continued his volunteer work driving the golf cart courtesy shuttle at the hospital. As a new Stephen Minister, he also volunteered three days a week in the evenings walking around the hospital and visiting with patients. "I get the list of patients in each room," says Tom. "If the door is closed, I don't go in. If the door is open I go in, but I don't walk in strong and start praying, I go in there to listen. I introduce myself as part of the Chaplain's group, telling them that I'm just there to say hello and see how they are doing." Tom says he just lets the conversation go where it leads. Sometimes it leads to a religious discussion, but Tom doesn't push the topic. "Getting that volunteer job was incredible," says Tom. "I have so many things to be thankful for. I could see it, and I knew God was making me the luckiest person in the world. I just felt blessed and very thankful."

When Tom learned through his Stephen Ministry leader that male volunteers were needed to assist with a grief ministry, he didn't hesitate to volunteer. Little did he realize that the fourteen-week class Tom came prepared to help with actually helped him process his grief over losing Karen. "Attending the grief class was good for me, because I don't think I fully grieved while dealing with the divorce," says Tom. "Going through the class, I thought a lot about Karen." At the same time, Tom also attended a divorce support group at the same church. Tom says he felt good after he completed the grief and divorce support groups.

With the comfort of a stable job in place, Tom felt secure in moving out of his apartment and into a rental home. With the help of a friend, Tom found a great house, but shortly upon moving in he discovered a broken faucet resulting in a call to his new landlord. When she arrived, Tom found it very easy to talk to her, and he felt a mutual attraction between the two of them. He extended a dinner invitation to her, and Maureen accepted. "I had to move on," says Tom. "There is no doubt in my mind that this was another situation where God was in control. Maureen is a Christian. It is just incredible. It was such a great week, because I got a promotion at work, met someone very special to me, and learned that Sarah's plans to move meant only moving thirty minutes away, keeping my kids close by. It was the last piece of the puzzle."

Maureen and Tom dated steadily and within just a few months knew a wedding was imminent. In March 2009, at a wedding chapel in Lake Tahoe, they exchanged wedding vows and became husband and wife. Tom's kids instantly loved Maureen, and life felt good once again for him. They began their marriage strong with God at the center, and Tom knew that God would be the key to keeping it that way. They would be challenged with problems brought into the marriage from both their pasts, but through all the trials God brought them closer together and kept them on a firm foundation.

As Tom reflects over the past four years of his life, he never imagined at the age of forty that he would have experienced the death of a child, loss of a job, DUI, divorce, loss of in-laws, loss of friends, and loss of a home. But, Tom says he is closer to God than he's ever been before. He admits it was a slow process but realizes there was not one step in the entire process that didn't go perfectly, including the DUI. Tom's pivotal circumstances became a divine opportunity for God to work in him in order that He might work through him. Tom's ministry at the hospital is just one example.

On a typical night, Tom takes a printed list of all the patients in the hospital, sits down in the lobby to review it, and plans out his volunteer time based upon the information on the list. He groups the patients by floor, and then looks at the number of days they have been in the hospital as well as their ages. In particular, he looks for people in single rooms who don't have a lot of family with them.

Tom recalls one particular day's rounds, which included a visit with an older lady. She was milling around her husband's room watching him as he peacefully slept in the bed. The sleeping patient was a retired minister and was being released the next day to hospice at the assisted living facility where he came from. She was thankful for that care, because she could no longer care for him at home. She was a sweet lady with a love for God that flowed from her countenance, despite the situation. Tom talked with her and prayed with her, and left feeling more blessed by the visit than the lady he set out to bless.

Next door to the minister was a young guy watching sports. He had his spleen removed when he was young, so any time he developed a fever it was serious and usually landed him in the hospital. He had no family nearby to visit him and seemed lonely. All of his family was in Florida except his girlfriend who was home attending to their seven-month-old. He was chatty and easy to talk to, and just thankful for a visit. He was hoping they could get his blood count under control so he could go home. Tom didn't have to say things like a minister might say with scripture or words of spiritual encouragement. All these people wanted was to know that someone cared enough about them to stop by and check on them, and Tom was the perfect candidate. Tom asked if he could pray with the man, and with a smile on his face he graciously accepted the offer.

Next on his tour, Tom visited the orthopedic floor where he met a female patient with a cast on her arm. Without waiting for Tom to inquire, she quickly explained how she fell off a ladder getting Christmas decorations and broke her shoulder, arm, leg, and foot necessitating multiple surgeries. She shared how her husband was not as excited about decorating as she was, and in her impatience she tried to do it all herself. Again, Tom just listened and allowed her to tell her story. Tom's visits were not viewed as an intrusion but rather a blessing.

Tom's last stop that night would be the Intensive Care Unit where nurses directed him to a family in the waiting room in dire need of a visit. There he found a mom worried sick over her son's life hanging in the balance. He was breathing at five to ten percent of his lung capacity and things were very serious. During a forty-five-minute visit with her in the waiting area, she shared her personal struggles with family members—struggles that were creating difficulties in making important treatment decisions for her sick son. She shared about her own ministry to help others and about her job. Tom could have sat there for hours with her just sharing life. He ended in prayer for her son, as well as for the relationship issues dividing the family over this gravely ill family member.

Walking into strangers' hospital rooms or in a hospital family waiting area and just striking up a conversation would not fall in most people's comfort zone, but God had equipped Tom through his heart-breaking loss to minister to others in this way. His ministry to others is such an encouragement of how God brings good out of someone's personal pain. Tom was touching lives with every hospital visit he made. Words didn't have to be preached. People could see and feel the love of God through his work, his touch, his words, and his time.

Who, besides God, could have ever predicted the event in Tom's life and the magnitude of the influence it would have on his life in this world and his spiritual life? His tragic loss was the catalyst for a major life change, a change Tom would not have signed up for, but a change he is now thankful for – a change God leveraged and used to grow his faith BIG. Tom could have looked at his circumstances and walked farther away from God, blaming him for the tragedy that took place. Instead, he ran to God and discovered the love that had always been there just waiting for him to embrace. That day in 2005 may have begun as just another average day, but to Tom it has become a day that defines who he is and whose he is, and his life will never be the same again.

Regret
Rev. Haas

There is a place in Jamaica called the Land of Looking Behind. Its history dates back to 1655, when the English invaded the Spanish-settled island, and indigenous slaves from sugar plantations fled to a remote, inhospitable area called Cockpit Country. This area, which is surrounded by the lush, verdant island, is actually a star-shaped limestone valley…a very dry, barren and hostile land. It was through this desolate area that the slaves fled from their Spanish plantation bosses when the English invaded. The treacherous terrain caused many of them to get lost or injured, and many died along the way. As the slaves fled, they constantly looked back behind them to see if the plantation owners were pursuing them. Those who slowed down enough to be captured were put to death for trying to escape. Others stumbled and fell over the sharp-edged cliffs to their death because they were running with their heads turned away from holes and obstacles. And so the area became known as the dangerous Land of Looking Behind, and you can still find it on ancient maps of Jamaica. Looking behind meant peril, injury and death.

So much of the grief process involves looking behind. But looking behind can be fatal in our grief process as well. While it is a natural reaction to spend time reflecting on the relationship we have experienced with the person who has died, many people find themselves in a cycle of regret. We regret not spending enough time with them; we regret things we said; we regret things we didn't say; and it is easy to find ourselves stuck in a place of looking behind.

Many people experience a bad case of the IfonlyI'ds…If only I had made him get a checkup earlier, if only I had been there when she died, if only I had left five minutes earlier, we'd have missed the drunk driver, etc. People stuck in regret construct lists of things they should have done differently, or did wrong or didn't do at all, that they regret. This can be especially hard on those who were estranged at the time of death, as the overwhelming finality of death presents no opportunities to relieve the guilt they carry by allowing them to reconcile. The problem with IfonlyI'ds is that they have no resolution and will drive you crazy in the meantime.

In biblical terms we call these "lamentations." Lamenting has been a common response to regret since the beginning of time. Jeremiah wrote the Book of Lamentations when the temple in Jerusalem fell in 586BC. The Israelites found themselves facing a city in ruins and they fled to exile and entered into Babylonian slavery. It was understood that the temple and their nation had been destroyed because of their sin. The regret they experienced over having disobeyed God was expressed in five poems, as Jeremiah acknowledges and rues their national sin. See the visions of regret that arise from these words:

> *The elders of the Daughter of Zion sit on the ground in silence;*
> *they have sprinkled dust on their heads and put on sackcloth.*
> *The young women of Jerusalem have bowed their heads to the*
> *ground. (Lamentations 2:10, NIV 1984)*

The suffering they experienced was recorded along with their regret. Jeremiah describes a portrait of a widow crying in the night with no one to comfort her as she regrets her disobedience:

> *"This is why I weep and my eyes overflow with tears. No one is*
> *near to comfort me, no one to restore my spirit. My children are*
> *destitute because the enemy has prevailed."*

Zion stretches out her hands, but there is no one to comfort her. The LORD has decreed for Jacob that his neighbors become his foes; Jerusalem has become an unclean thing among them.

"The LORD is righteous, yet I rebelled against his command. Listen, all you peoples; look upon my suffering. My young men and maidens have gone into exile.

"I called to my allies but they betrayed me. My priests and my elders perished in the city while they searched for food to keep themselves alive.

"See, O LORD, how distressed I am! I am in torment within, and in my heart I am disturbed, for I have been most rebellious. Outside, the sword bereaves; inside, there is only death. (Lamentations 2:16-20, NIV 1984)*

The lamentations of the people gave form and words to the deep suffering and pain they were experiencing. The intensity of their suffering cannot be overstated; the slaying of children, carnage, sacrilege and cannibalism marked the desperate loss of respect for human worth.

Suffering has always been a part of our human condition, and until Christ comes again, always will. People in the midst of grief understand suffering in ways they have never experienced before. Lamentations attempts neither to explain suffering nor to offer a step-by-step remedy. It simply speaks to the pain, keeping company with the sufferers, and points toward God as He enters into it with us.

Hear these words of encouragement from Lamentations:

God's loyal love couldn't have run out,
His merciful love couldn't have dried up.
They're created new every morning.
How great your faithfulness!
I'm sticking with God (I say it over and over)
He's all I've got left.
God proves to be good to the man who passionately waits,
To the woman who diligently seeks.
It's a good thing to quietly hope,
Quietly hope for help from God.
It's a good thing when you're young
To stick it out through the hard times.
When life is heavy and hard to take,
Go off by yourself. Enter the silence.
Bow in prayer. Don't ask questions:
Wait for hope to appear.
Don't run from trouble. Take it full-force.
The "worst" is never the worst.
Why?
Because the Master won't ever walk out and fail to return.
(Lamentations 3: 22-33, The Message)

Note again that this passage comes in the midst of the complete devastation of a society who is filled with deep regret over their actions and inactions, yet these words reflect no 'looking behind.' Instead the counsel is "go off by yourself. Enter the silence, bow in prayer, don't ask questions and WAIT FOR HOPE TO APPEAR."

The problem with regret is that it is a rock concert of pure cacophonous noise played at unbearable decibels. It is a place of shouting that bounces around in our heads, yelling at us like Marine sergeants. Always accusing, always finding fault, always destructive, regret spends its time lamenting while looking out the rear-view mirror.

What a terrible way to drive a life.

This passage invites us to re-focus our attention to the front windshield and wait for hope to appear. Just as God's merciful and loyal love are created new every morning, so to must we begin to move ahead in expectation that peace and hope will be created in us new every morning. Mourning and morning may sound alike, but the similarity ends there. The land of looking behind is yesterday. Regret comes in the mourning. Hope comes in the morning.

Why? Because the Master won't ever walk out and fail to return.

The death of a loved one can feel as though the Master has just walked out. While we regret our own inaction, we can agonize over His. Why didn't He save my father? Why did He let my child die? Why didn't He bring a miracle? Our regrets aren't only our own; we regret the feeling that the Master walked out on us in our hour of greatest need.

But the Master won't ever walk out and fail to return, even when he died on the cross.

This was the greatest lesson Peter learned in his brief time with Jesus. Peter is a favorite disciple of many because he is so like us: enthusiastic, distracted, passionate, prone to say the wrong thing, and he let down the people he loved the most. We might imagine, as he was following Jesus into the Garden of Gethsemane that last night of Jesus' life, the last thing on his mind was abandoning his friend, master and teacher. Nothing in his previous relationship with the Lord would have led us toward that moment. Yet betray Him he did, as he denied not once, not twice but three times even knowing Jesus.

What Peter may have been experiencing is a matter of pure speculation, but one has to wonder—perhaps he feared that the Master was about to walk out and fail to return. As he saw the Roman soldiers accosting Him and taking him away, perhaps in that moment his faith in Jesus' divinity failed, and he contemplated the idea that He would never return.

Can you even fathom his regret? Can you imagine the dismay he felt? Can you see how he must have spent each moment from that point looking behind?

—Until he saw Christ again.

After the crucifixion, the disciples returned to their normal work of fishing. They went to the Sea of Galilee and fished all night, catching nothing. In the morning a fellow on the shore called out to them to cast their net over the other side of the boat. When they did, they caught a boatload of fish! Instantly Peter knew it must be Jesus.

Peter jumped into the water to swim to his Master. The rest of the disciples followed in the fish-filled boat. On shore they feasted on a breakfast of Messiah-grilled grouper on toast, recognizing Jesus in the breaking of the bread and of the fish. Then Peter finally had the moment that wiped away his regret forever:

John 21

> *When they had finished eating, Jesus said to Simon Peter, "Simon son of John, do you truly love me more than these?"*
> *"Yes, Lord," he said, "you know that I love you."*
> *Jesus said, "Feed my lambs."*
>
> *Again Jesus said, "Simon son of John, do you truly love me?"*
> *He answered, "Yes, Lord, you know that I love you."*
> *Jesus said, "Take care of my sheep."*
>
> *The third time he said to him, "Simon son of John, do you love me?" Peter was hurt because Jesus asked him the third time, "Do*

you love me?" He said, "Lord, you know all things; you know that I love you."

Jesus said, "Feed my sheep."

I tell you the truth, when you were younger you dressed yourself and went where you wanted; but when you are old you will stretch out your hands, and someone else will dress you and lead you where you do not want to go."

Jesus said this to indicate the kind of death by which Peter would glorify God. Then he said to him, "Follow me!" (John 21:15-19, NIV 1984)

Having given over his regret to Jesus, having expressed his love for the Lord, Peter was now equipped to obediently follow Jesus, and become the cornerstone of the church. He left the Land of Looking Behind and was able to claim his future with hope.

That same offer is being made to you right now. Jesus stands before you as he did Peter and wants to know one thing: Do you love me? If you love him, lay down your regret and offer him your life. He will fold that regret into tiny little squares until poof, it flies from his hand like magician's paper.

Recently a church sign in North Carolina had the following message:
Sorrow looks behind;
Worry looks around;
Faith looks up.

Quit looking down; quit looking behind. It's time to look up and wait for hope to appear.

CHAPTER SIX

Michael

Michael's phone rang at 5 a.m. on August 23, 2006—a day he will never forget. He could feel the panic from his dad's voice flow through his veins as his heart began to beat faster. His dad managed to utter the words through his broken voice that Michael's mom had suddenly passed away. She was found slumped over in her favorite knitting chair—a place she would often go in the middle of the night to knit or read when insomnia set in. What had happened? She wasn't sick and had even recently endured several pre-operative tests before some routine foot surgery, and everything checked out fine. An autopsy would reveal that Michael's mom died of heart failure at the age of sixty-six. "It was a bit of a shock," said Michael. "I wasn't ready. I don't think you can ever be ready." Longevity ran in his mom's side of the family. In fact, Michael's grandmother is in her 90s.

Married with nine-month-old twins, Michael was not only unable to face the loss of his mother, known as "Mema," but he also could not imagine how the loss would impact the grandkids. However, his inner voice was telling him that there were many reasons why he should not be feeling this immense grief. *I've been moved out of the house for fifteen years. I have my own family now, kids, and a job,* he thought. *What's wrong with me?* Six days after his mother passed away, Michael gathered up the courage to pick up the phone and inquire about a grief support program at a local church. He was trying to be proactive. When a deacon at his church told him not to be shy about seeking help for his grief, he put aside the stigma that was often attached to a support group and took that first courageous step towards healing. Michael was hesitant though, thinking that he might be out of place attending such a group. *I'm just grieving over my mom, and people who have lost a spouse have it harder, because they face going home every night to an empty bed and an empty house,* he thought.

Michael admitted his acceptance of his mother's death and the fact he would never get to call or see her holding one of his twins again, but expressed having trouble dealing with the immense sadness and sense of loss he carried around. "This is the first time I have ever had to deal with the loss of someone close to me," he says. Michael agreed to attend the next grief support group meeting, which was a huge step, especially for a thirty-four-year-old male.

Filled with anxiety and worry about what would happen when he walked into that first meeting, seeing unfamiliar faces in an unfamiliar place, Michael sat in his car outside the church, preparing and rehearsing what he would say. *If I open my mouth there might be a bunch of tears and I'll get all emotional,* he thought. *I have no idea what to expect.* After all, in our culture today, men aren't supposed to cry. They slap you on the back and tell you to just handle your grief and get over it. Michael nervously made it into the church building and sat through the entire meeting, without uttering a word. "I didn't say anything. I was too nervous so I just listened," he recalls. Michael left with a new perspective—it was necessary and normal to feel the way he did and that he wasn't taking his grief too hard. "The biggest thing I got from silently listening to others in the group share was that I'm not crazy," he declared. "It helped me understand how silly it was to think my grief was insignificant."

It took Michael three meetings to finally utter a word and begin opening his vulnerable male heart to share his personal story of loss.

"The support group was good by itself when I was just listening, but sharing opened up new doors. I mean it was a totally different experience after that. Everyone there can relate to what you're saying. That's what floored me about it – I'm not weird and I'm not going crazy."

Upon finishing the 14-week grief support group, Michael shared how God was using his mother's death as a catalyst for personal growth and spiritual renewal. Nothing is sweeter to my ears than to hear the good news when God transforms lives through grief. "The changes in me as a person since August 23, 2006, have been profound," Michael exclaimed. He went on to explain the many areas of his life that were impacted through his loss.

The first change was his job and family. Before she passed away, Michael's mom keenly observed his work habits and felt he was a borderline workaholic. Being a mother, she felt it her motherly duty to bring it to his attention and begged him to slow down at work. Only after losing his mother did Michael learn that lesson. Now he resists the pressures his bosses place upon him and makes spending quality time with his wife and kids a top priority. Michael also became very conscious of how much he and his wife bickered and argued before his mother's death. Realizing how precious life is and how our days on earth are numbered, Michael's perspective changed on how ridiculous it was to be angry over issues like who put the dishes in the dishwasher wrong. Unable to draw comfort from other family members who were in denial, Michael drew closer to his wife during the process, and she became his main source of comfort. With this change in priorities, Michael began to put things in the proper perspective, and he could sense a complete shift in his relationship with his wife—and it felt amazing.

The second and most profound change was Michael's relationship with the Lord. "Spiritually, I made a 180-degree turn. It never occurred to me we were all going to die, which was silly," Michael admitted. "Dying was always something that happened to someone else. While I had always professed faith in God and His mysteries, I realized that I had never equated death and the afterlife with my faith. I went to Mass because I was supposed to and prayed because the priest said it was time to." Michael had a difficult time thinking of his mom in Heaven even though she was a deeply spiritual woman grounded with her faith in God. The grief came out of nowhere, which sent him searching for answers. Where did he turn? "I couldn't find any answers until I decided to crack open the Bible," Michael said. "It had been ten years since I had opened one." Like most who have been absent from the word, Michael didn't know where in the world to start.

One Sunday after attending Mass, he decided to dust off his Bible and open to the chapter where the Sunday Mass reading came from. Realizing God's word was moving him in a way like never before, Michael thirsted for more. When he was younger, Michael read the Bible for educational purposes, but now he was slowly drawing comfort from the Word during this journey through grief and experiencing God in an amazing and eye-opening way. His favorite book was Psalms because Michael could identify and draw comfort from the authors, like mentors, each facing struggles similar to his filled with questions and doubt. "I have a long way to go in this arena, but at least I am now walking the path. I am very much the son from the parable of the prodigal son, on my way home," he analyzed. "I sometimes felt it was ironic that mom always wanted me to get closer to God, and I never did—and then when I did begin my new journey, she was gone."

Shortly after his mother's death, while he was struggling to accept the finality of it, Michael would wake up each morning, look at his wristwatch, and wonder if it was August 23, 2006. Was his mind tricking him into thinking that maybe he dreamed his mother's death? However, after Michael began spending time reading the Bible, a transformative process began to happen that proved difficult for him to articulate. Michael said, "It was weird how it rushed over me. It was almost like a hand resting on my shoulder. I thought it was interesting so I decided to pray before bed that night because it helped me sleep." More amazing is what happened the next morning. The usual routine of glancing at his watch and doubting the reality of the situation suddenly ceased and the loss of his mother was not his first thought upon waking. Michael was seeking God and God was providing exactly what he needed. Michael was beginning to sense something going on which prompted questions like, "Why is this? Where am I drawing this comfort? What are the meanings behind these things I'm reading? It kind of spiraled and is still going on," he said. Michael says that his priest likened the grief process to a marathon and not a 100-yard dash and Michael agrees, now feeling much better about the length of the journey he is on.

Michael also made a new commitment to live a healthier life in response to his mother's passing. Michael always thought he was young and tough and didn't need to waste time going to useless doctor appointments, so he didn't. Even with a family history that included a grandfather dying of a massive heart attack, a dad with high cholesterol, and a mom with high blood pressure, Michael still didn't feel it necessary to make annual doctor visits a priority. His mother had urged him to get a checkup long ago, but as usual he turned a deaf ear to her loving, motherly advice. After her death, Michael learned that the last discussion his mom had with his brother regarded Michael's health and her desire for him to be more proactive. Her death motivated him to do what he stubbornly refused to do before—make that appointment for a checkup, ensuring he'd be healthy for his wife and children. During his checkup, the only thing the doctor expressed concern over was Michael's weight, and he immediately began working on it. It was also time to schedule an appointment for a surgical procedure he had been putting off. Eating better and daily exercise became part of his new health and fitness plan. Michael began running three and a half miles a day, six days a week, in order to meet a personal goal. "I'm going to enter a program to start getting into a marathon. It's always been a goal of mine but I put it off. One day I'd like to say I've run a marathon—maybe a triathlon," dreams Michael.

On July 4, 2007, Michael's dream would come true as he competed in Atlanta's Peachtree Road Race and achieved his goal to finish the entire race. He set his sights on the 2008 race and his goal of finishing in under an hour. The new eating and exercise plan also resulted in a new, slimmer Michael. With this effort, he lost forty pounds and felt great.

As Michael looks back upon his grief journey and reflects on why he grew and how it happened, he recalls that it was the result of a combination of several factors. "That first moment when I began talking in the grief group was as defining as when I opened the Bible in terms of a change for the better. It was a real rocky road there for the first couple of months and when those two things happened at the same time I saw the light at the end of the tunnel. I never really thought about the plan, God's plan. There is a lot going on that I'll never understand and I'm not meant to understand. I can't help but think that God intended for some of the side effects of mom's passing to be the resulting positive changes in my life, like trying to be a better husband and father, trying to be there more often, being less severe at work and having patience to allow co-workers to do things their own unique way. I can't help but think that's part of the plan too. And,

I know now, deep in my heart, that mom is smiling her broad smile seeing me become this person."

God transformed Michael in a mighty way. When Michael embraced his faith and began to seek out God's word after so many years of silence, God opened all the doors and it was good! There wasn't much God didn't change in Michael's life. When we seek out God in our times of suffering and allow Him to change us through our pain, there is no limit to what He can do.

Weakness
Rev. Haas

Oh, how we hate to admit our weaknesses. The secular world despises weakness in any form. See how many "Celebrity Apprentice," "Biggest Loser," and "Survivor- type" shows emphasize the strong triumphing over the weak. From birth we are trained to run faster, jump higher and push harder than the other kids on the playground. We teach our sons to "man up" and tell them "only sissies cry." We teach our daughters not to be crybabies, as though weakness is a character flaw. When we grow from childhood to adulthood, we see weakness as a tremendous failure and something that needs to be denied and repressed. Our weaknesses embarrass us.

And so when weakness enters into our lives as the unwanted companion of grief, we shy away from it, denying its intrusion, ignoring its presence and steadfastly protesting that we are strong enough to bear it all! Stoically, we thrust out our lower lip, made rigid by sheer obstinacy, and refuse all help and support. We turn down offers of meals, funeral planning, help around the house, friends lending a sympathetic ear....after all, we don't need help. We're strong enough. We can handle this. And we do this at our peril.

In dealing with the normal and universal feelings of weakness that accompany grief, it is helpful for us to think about Jesus in the Garden of Gethsemane on the night before he died. On this night, He was possibly at the weakest point of his life. As you examine this passage, consider the idea that He may have been even weaker in this moment than on the cross.

Jesus and his disciples have shared the last supper together in the Upper Room, and now it's nearly midnight as they leave and descend to the streets of the city. They pass the Lower Pool and exit through the Fountain Gate, walking out of the city of Jerusalem. The roads were lined with the smoking fires and tents of the visiting Passover Pilgrims. They pass through the valley and ascend up the rocky path that takes them up the Mount of Olives to a garden known as Gethsemane.

The road to the Gethsemane is steep, so they probably stop to rest. Jesus must have stopped and looked back over the city of Jerusalem before he began his final ascent to the garden. When he reaches the entry, he stops and turns his eyes toward his circle of friends. It will be the last time he sees them before they abandon him. In a short while, the soldiers will arrive and each one will flee; they all will betray him. And so He enters the Garden.

Let's pause for a moment here and look closer at the Garden of Gethsemane, since that is where grief has also delivered us. Jesus experienced weakness in the Garden, and in our own gardens we too are struggling with our weaknesses. What can the Garden teach us?

First of all, the Garden of Gethsemane is not really a garden per se, but an orchard of olive trees. Olive trees still grow there today. During Jesus' day it was a place of business, and its olive press produced the local areas' supply of oil. This is where the word Gethsemane comes in… a *gat* (Hebrew) is a press, made up of a large five-foot-high square stone pillar and a trough, and a *semane*, or seman is oil. Thus Gethsemane means, "press of oil."

The olive oil workers would spend the day gathering olives and placing them in woven fishnet-like bags. They would bring the bags to the press and put them on top of a stone table specially designed for oil production. This table was round with edges that curved downward to a trough all around the base. The trough is angled so that it funnels its contents into a large pot that holds the oil. The trough is designed to receive the "Geth's semane." A tall square stone is lifted up and set on top of the bag, and for several hours its tremendous weight is left there to crush the liquid from the olive. The enormous weight of the stone literally crushes the oil from the olives.

And so it is no mistake that Jesus spent his last night in the Garden of Gethsemane. From there he would leave to go to the cross and receive the enormous weight of the world. He took upon Himself the Gethsemane of our sins, which like an enormous stone, crushed the blood of the atonement right from His body until it ran down the cross to the world below.

Knowing what is to come, listen now to what Jesus says to HIS Father in His weakest moment of deepest despair as recorded in Matthew 26:

> *Then Jesus went with his disciples to a place called Gethsemane, and he said to them, "Sit here while I go over there and pray." He took Peter and the two sons of Zebedee along with him, and he began to be sorrowful and troubled. Then he said to them, "My soul is overwhelmed with sorrow to the point of death. Stay here and keep watch with me." Going a little farther, he fell with his face to the ground and prayed, "My Father, if it is possible, may this cup be taken from me. Yet not as I will, but as you will." Then he returned to his disciples and found them sleeping. "Could you men not keep watch with me for one hour?" he asked Peter. "Watch and pray so that you will not fall into temptation. The spirit is willing, but the body is weak." He went away a second time and prayed, "My Father, if it is not possible for this cup to*

be taken away unless I drink it, may your will be done." When
he came back, he again found them sleeping, because their eyes
were heavy. So he left them and went away once more and prayed
the third time, saying the same thing. Then he returned to the
disciples and said to them, "Are you still sleeping and resting?
Look, the hour is near, and the Son of Man is betrayed into
the hands of sinners. Rise, let us go! Here comes my betrayer!"
(Matthew 26:36-46, NIV 1984)

The cup Jesus speaks of is an Old Testament reference to the cup of
wrath; the wrath that would be poured on him the moment he took
on the sin of the world. That would be the moment when, for the
first time in his pre-existence, he would experience something that he
dreaded with all of his heart—separation from God. Sin is separation.
Taking on sin meant He could not be part of the Father.

And so He knew that when He climbed upon the cross, He would
be separated from the Father. This knowledge was something He
couldn't bear in His last hours, and so in the garden of that agony,
he asked for the cup of wrath to be taken from him. Three times,
he pleaded with His Father, "Take this cup from me." Not because
he was afraid of the beatings, not because he was afraid of pain, and
certainly not because he was afraid of death, but because he was
horrified at the thought of being apart from His Father.

Yet even in his weakest moment, as he prayed in agony for the third
time with drops of blood beading on His forehead, He looked up
through the gnarled olive trees toward the starry night of eternity
and do you know what He saw? He saw you.

He saw you in your own garden of agony…he saw you in a body that
would feel weary and exhausted, and a heart that grows weak. He
saw you lost and confused, even betrayed by your friends. He saw you

staring into the pit of your own failures, trapped by your sin, defeated by death. He saw you in your present grief, and He was filled with compassion.

There you were, in your own Garden of Gethsemane, and He didn't want you to be forever alone. And so after the third prayer, and after seeing you and choosing what was to come for your sake, his prayer brought him peace, and he followed through for you.

And because he pushed through his weakness and drank from the cup of wrath, you and the rest of the world were saved.

Many of us are in a dark place of Gethsemane. We feel like we are trapped in an oil press where an immense stone of grief, uncertainty, anger, financial struggles or despair is suddenly crushing the life out of us. We feel that we don't know where to turn or how much longer we can endure this crushing. What can Jesus' experience in his own Gethsemane say to us to give us hope and comfort?

We must begin where He began...by turning to the Father. In the Greek, Jesus uses the word "Abba," which The Message translates as "Papa." In this choice of words, Jesus reveals the nature of the relationship He shares with God. We don't get an image of a patriarchal authority, which surely God is, but rather a close, personal, intimate parent-child bond. It causes us to consider, what is my relationship with God like? Is He a Papa to me? Can I turn to him with such ease and familiarity?

Remember that we see in the scriptures again and again how Jesus would remove himself from his day to spend time with his Papa. This teaches us that a bond this close can only be the result of daily interaction. Daily scripture reading, daily devotionals, daily meditation and of course, daily prayer are all ways to come to know the Father as Abba-Papa.

And so like Jesus, we must pray. Pray fervently, pray earnestly and pray with consistency. Notice the pattern of Jesus' prayer in this passage; first he calls upon His relationship with God. Next he acknowledges God's power and sovereignty; "You can take this cup away." Third, he prays the desire of his heart; "Remove this cup from me." And finally he submits to God's will; "But not my will be done, Father, but Your will be done."

Here is the model of Jesus' Gethsemane prayer:

1. Call upon God as your Father, your Abba-Papa.

2. Acknowledge God's power and sovereignty over your grief.

3. Pray the desire of your heart to be freed of your sorrow.

4. Submit your prayer to God's will.

Notice that Jesus skips a step, one that we must include; he omits the confession of sin. He couldn't include that because He himself was without sin.

And the Scriptures are very clear that He prayed the same prayer three times in a row. Think of a person felling a large oak tree; they may take hundreds of swings of the ax to the trunk before finally one last blow causes the tree to fall. It's not the last chop that fells the tree, but all the chops that lead up to the last one. In the same way we are reminded to be persistent in prayer. See what Paul says in his letter to Thessalonica:

> "*Rejoice always; pray without ceasing; in everything give thanks; for this is God's will for you in Christ Jesus.*" (1 Thessalonians 5:16-18, New American Standard Translation)

And again in Ephesians:

> *"With all prayer and petition pray at all times in the Spirit, and with this in view, be on the alert with all perseverance and petition for all the saints."* (Ephesians 6:18, New Living Translation)

And if you are so weak that you can't even figure out what to pray, and you can't make any words form in your mouth or your mind when you kneel, Romans 8:26 reminds us to take heart:

> *"And the Holy Spirit helps us in our weakness. For example, we don't know what God wants us to pray for. But the Holy Spirit prays for us with groaning that cannot be expressed in words."* (Romans 8:26, New Living Translation)

But perhaps Paul's best counsel about weakness comes from this passage in 2 Corinthians, Chapter 12: 8-10. In his letter to the church in Corinth, he is telling them about a "thorn in his flesh" that he had asked God to take away. We don't know exactly what the "thorn" was; scholars speculate that it was perhaps and illness, a physical impairment or handicap, a person who opposed him, or even the Jews who were confronting him about his beliefs. Whatever the thorn, God had not removed it, allowing Paul to discover this about himself and his Lord:

> *"Three different times I begged the Lord to take it away. Each time he said, "My grace is all you need. My power works best in weakness." So now I am glad to boast about my weaknesses, so that the power of Christ can work through me. That's why I take pleasure in my weaknesses, and in the insults, hardships, persecutions, and troubles that I suffer for Christ. For when I am weak, then I am strong."* (2 Corinthians 12:8-10, New Living Translation)

Did you see it? God's grace is enough. God's grace is sufficient. Your weakness allows God's grace to work through you. Your weakness makes you strong. Praise God!

Chris Tomlin wrote these beautiful words in a contemporary praise song called, "Your Grace is Enough." Use these words as your prayer, as you acknowledge your weakness and ask God for His strength.

> *Your grace is enough! Heaven reaching down to us!*
> *Your grace is enough for me;*
> *God, I see your grace is enough; I'm covered in your love,*
> *Your grace is enough for me!*

For me. And for you. In the crushing of your Gethsemane, His grace is enough. In your loneliness, His grace is enough. In the depths of your sorrow, His grace is enough. In your weakest moment, reach out and find him, for His grace is enough. Amen.

CHAPTER SEVEN

Ann

Ann Watson's favorite word these days is "providence." Providence is defined in Christian terms as the foreseeing care and guidance of God over the creatures of the earth; it points to God who directs the affairs of humankind with wise benevolence. Providence—a strange and amazing word for a woman who watched her husband slowly die of brain cancer.

A mutual friend introduced Ann to Ron Watson while Ann was attending Mercer University and Ron, a student at Georgia State. Following Ann's graduation, Ron continued on to law school. The heartbreaking separation led Ann to pack up her belongings and move to Atlanta, closer to her *soul mate*, as she lovingly refers to Ron. Following a six-year courtship, Ron finally dropped to one knee and proposed. Next came the picture-perfect wedding, a job offer for Ron with a law firm, the purchase of their very first home, and a new baby boy named Troy.

Ann married with the expectation that she and Ron would follow the same spiritual path of her family and attend church together. She grew up surrounded by family members with visibly strong faith, but Ron, however, did not. That was an important topic the couple made sure to address prior to marriage. Ron had agreed to support Ann's faith although he didn't buy into Christianity the way Ann embraced it. He saw it as a place for his kids to have fun, a social outlet that teaches morals—seeing its benefits in a cognitive way. Once married their religious plans fell flat, and they never set foot in a church. "When Troy came along, we still didn't go to church, and then our second child, Lisa, came along, and we still didn't go to church," says Ann. "My whole family would be praying for us to raise our kids in the Christian faith and would ask if we'd been to church." Ann was annoyed by their persistent inquisitions, because deep in her heart she knew without a doubt they were right and she was wrong. Ann explains, "My faith had been laying underneath the romance of a husband, a baby, and buying a house, and God just wasn't in the forefront for me until December 15, 2001."

After tucking the kids into bed that December night, Ann seized the quiet moment of a peaceful house and telephoned Ron's stepmom from their living room where Ron was changing a ceiling light bulb. Her phone call was abruptly halted when Ron lost his balance stepping down off a chair, tumbled into the Christmas tree, and then smacked his head on the wooden window ledge. In sheer panic, Ann dropped the phone, which fell apart upon impact with the floor and rushed over to Ron. He could only stare at her, unable to utter a single word. Ron was also unable to move his right arm or leg making it impossible for Ann to move him off the floor.

With adrenaline flowing, Ann re-assembled the pieces of the phone and dialed 9-1-1. Neighbors were alerted upon hearing the loud sirens of rescue vehicles. She recalls, "My next door neighbor, James Croft, rushed over thinking maybe one of the kids was hurt." James, a fire department captain and trained paramedic, waited with Ann while decisions were being made, and then chauffeured her to the local municipal airport and then to the trauma hospital where Ron was transported via helicopter thirty miles away. "My first thought was a stroke, but symptoms started to dissipate," says Ann. "Ron regained the use of his arm and could communicate through slurred speech, but we still were concluding it was a stroke."

Four days later, still lying in the trauma hospital, doctors noticed strange, erratic movement in Ron's eyes leading them to schedule an MRI. It was now December 22nd, and while the world rushed out to purchase last-minute holiday gifts, the thought of Christmas cheer was the farthest thing from the Watson's mind. On December 23rd following the MRI, Ann and Ron received a visit from the neurosurgeon, a visit that Ann refers to as "the punt—when someone else comes in to drop the big, bad news on you." The news delivered by the brain surgeon was, "You've got a brain stem tumor. If the brain is property, this is Manhattan, the most valuable property, not where you want a tumor to be. We can't remove it, and we can't biopsy it without the risk of paralysis or sending Ron into a possible vegetative state."

Ann's family, all present at the hospital to hear the neurosurgeon's results, quietly stepped out of the room giving Ann and Ron a moment alone to soak in the devastating news. At that moment, Ann cut to the chase and said to Ron, "There's only one way I can handle this and that's with God, and I need to know where you are." Ron could not come up with a response, so when Ann left that evening to go home Ron was left wrestling with a life-changing decision. Ron later told Ann it was the blackest, darkest night of his life. He thought he was going to die, he wasn't sure about God, and he didn't know where to start to figure it out.

Ann was convinced her upbringing in a strong Christian family had laid the groundwork that would enable her to boldly confront Ron about his beliefs. She was certain Ron had seen faith in action even if he didn't listen to what people said about faith. "My family is pretty up front and direct with their faith," says Ann. It's not something you wouldn't notice." Ann knew Ron, as part of the family, had observed the genuine faith acted out by every member of her family, especially her brother-in-law's. From the pastor who married them, to family, to other friends, Ann believed Ron saw God real in other people, preparing him for the moment when he would be at a life-altering crossroads deciding "is this real or is it not?"

Upon discharge from the hospital on Christmas Eve, friends and neighbors jumped into action. Knowing Ron was struggling with salvation and had no church to call home, James Croft arranged Ron a home visit with a pastor from his Methodist church. The pastor helped answer Ron's questions and put into perspective what beginning a relationship with Christ might look and feel like. In the following days, Ron also sought counsel from his long-time friend, Phil, who had re-prioritized his own life the year before. Ron wanted Phil to be the one to pray with him, so Ann invited Phil to dinner. Phil arrived with books in hand, but more importantly ready to pray the prayer of salvation should Ron desire. With friend Phil by his side, Ron humbly accepted Jesus Christ to be his Lord and Savior. Excited about his new relationship with God, the Watsons immediately started attending the local Methodist Church. There they met a young couple that shared a similar life experience and found the gift of a life-long friendship.

Ann remembers how amazing people were to them, "Ron's boss paid him for full-time work, people drove him to and from appointments, I had babysitting offers so I could be with Ron, and our Sunday school class literally adopted us. God provided me resources from day one. When we reached out to the church, there was never a moment that we weren't helped. There was never a time we didn't have some person through God's family helping us. I have such a debt of gratitude for the provisions we received. I really should be a servant to the church. Ron and I tried to find ways to give back, but there was no way I could repay what I was provided."

One person they had not counted on for help was Ron's mom, Mimi, because she was estranged from Ron and had no idea about the fall or the inoperable brain tumor. Mimi was even unaware her granddaughter, Lisa, had been born. At the time Ron was diagnosed, Ann and Ron decided to break the awkward silence and make a call to deliver the news. Ann recalls, "Mimi was devastated, of course, but immediately came back into our lives. Ron and his mom started what turned out to be an amazing restoration in their relationship." While Ron was on fire for God and shared that love with his mother, she was not so convinced about faith and Jesus. Ann and Ron had hoped that the way they lived their life with God at the center would have an affect on her as well. Ron loved to help in Sunday school, serve as an usher on Sunday mornings, and sing really loud to the wonderful music. "I'd be bumping him because he could only half hear, and he'd be louder than he realized and really off key," says Ann. "His mom was in the front row for all of that, but I don't know how much she took in."

Although surgery to remove the tumor was not an option, Ron chose to undergo six weeks of radiation therapy, hoping and praying for news that the tumor had shrunk. Amazing news arrived at Ron's post radiation checkup in spring 2002 – the tumor had shrunk to the point where they could hardly see it! As the shrunken tumor ceased putting pressure on Ron's brain, his speech returned almost immediately as well as the use of his right arm and leg. Doctors were so pleased with his condition that Ron's checkups were then scheduled annually. The only downside was the effects the treatments had on his body. Ron gained seventy-five pounds from the steroids he took, and he developed hearing loss from nerve damage due to radiation. The Watson's accepted those negative affects since it meant Ron was healed.

During treatment, Ann recalled how they halted any plans for the future, for the next Christmas, or for the next family vacation. "When you're in the place of a life-threatening illness, everything is so uncertain that it's very painful to plan for those future events." Ann says there were one or two scares along the road with Ron's vision, but they blamed it on the steroids and plowed ahead with life once again.

Feeling confident about his health, Ron decided to take a bold risk and open his own law practice. To ensure their bills were covered, Ann made a gut-wrenching decision to forego her favorite job as stay-at-home mom and seek full-time employment. "I grieved over that," says Ann. "It was a loss for me not to be home with my kids, but when an opportunity opened up at a local counseling office, my pastor's advice was to take it." The environment couldn't have been more perfect for Ann. It was a Christian counseling office, a full-time job, and was just what her family needed in many respects. Ann recalls, "It's a Christian group of people. How lucky could I be? I mean wow! How much more could God have provided an opportunity for me than to put me in a place like that?"

God provided for Ron as well by having his mom on board in the day-to-day operations of his new practice. Working together gave them the opportunity to catch up with each other, share life, and rebuild their broken relationship. Despite all his efforts, Ron's practice did not have the success he had hoped for, causing financial struggles for the family. The one thing he did have, though, was his health and his mom back in his life.

Mimi also helped out by picking up her granddaughter from preschool in the afternoons. One day, Lisa was left at pre-school anxiously waiting on the pick-up curb with no Mimi in sight. Ron knew something was terribly wrong when the preschool called to inform him nobody had come to get Lisa. He picked up Lisa and immediately headed to his mom's house. With no answer at the front door, Ron quickly ran through the grassy yard to gain entry through the back door. His heart sank when he found his mother on the floor dead from a heart attack at the age of fifty-five. This was a very traumatic event for him, recalls Ann. It seemed terribly unfair that just when Ron and Mimi had restored their broken relationship, she would pass away so unexpectedly.

Following the funeral, Ron had to sell his mother's house and sort out her personal belongings. He and Ann learned that the money they would inherit from her assets would financially change their lives, providing enough to clear Ron's medical bills, pay off other debt, and even take their children on a much-needed vacation to Walt Disney World. Ann credits God with providing them the resources for all of those blessings. She recalls leaving the magic of Disney in tears, reminiscing about the wonderful week they had just experienced as a family, "The fact that we had the money, the kids were the perfect age, and it was a perfect week—it was just a gift from Mimi that God provided." It was so good that Ann felt certain her joy would be interrupted with another setback somehow, somewhere.

A year later, just when things had settled down and were seemingly back to normal, Ron's vision began acting up again. "During his annual checkup in September 2007, the doctor waved us into a back room to view Ron's scans," says Ann. Their worst fears came true. The ugly tumor had returned. "I felt nauseous hearing the doctor tell us that Ron's tumor was definitely changing, slowly, but gradually." The only good news – chemotherapy, which had not been an option five years ago, was now finally available for this type of tumor.

The Watsons met with an oncologist to begin monthly chemotherapy treatments. The upside to his therapy was none of the usual hair loss, weight loss, or nausea, but the downside was the mammoth price tag of $2,000 per treatment. Ann stressed over how she would ever pay the high medical bills. Accepting the reality of their situation, they prepared to sell their beloved home and downsize to something more affordable.

Ann felt very blessed when a drug company grant provided funds for Ron's chemo, but she was blown away when an unassuming, humble woman from her church asked Ann's permission to explore an idea to help. Francis' idea was to somehow cover their mortgage payments for the next year until Ron was back on his feet. Francis took charge to set up a special account, worked with the church financial administrator, pooled funds from any willing donor, and paid Ann and Ron's monthly mortgage payment for fourteen months. However, Ron did not bounce back as planned, and just five months after re-diagnosis he suddenly went from being fine to sleeping all the time. Ron lost all his energy and stopped communicating with his family, a telltale sign that something was seriously wrong.

Needing time off from work to be with Ron, unselfish co-workers from Ann's counseling office stepped forward to donate their own vacation hours to Ann. One night in February 2008, Ann recalls Ron suddenly waking up and being unsure where the bathroom was. Concerned, Ann called Ron's family and told them they needed to come. Scrambling to prepare as quickly as possible, Ann was in dire need of a living will and power of attorney. Jack Jones, an attorney friend of Ron's, dropped everything and immediately drew up the necessary paperwork. To expedite things, Jack even met Ann and Ron in the parking lot of his office for signatures as they headed back to the hospital for more tests.

Ann had confided in a friend at church the previous Sunday that she was scared about the uncertainty of her future. That friend lovingly hugged Ann and gently whispered in her ear, "Are you ready?" Ann says it was God speaking to her through another person, because doctors would deliver the grim news the following week that Ron's tumor had more than tripled in size and gave him four to six weeks to live. "We had recently done a scan and no growth had been detected," says Ann. "Then suddenly he turned for the worse, just like that." Doctors told Ann it was time to break the news to her children, but first Ann had important questions for Ron while he was still coherent. She recalls, "We were sitting in the lab at the hospital, and I asked him how he wanted his life to end. I remember Ron's brother getting up and walking out of the room unable to handle the conversation. We talked about it – the funeral and who he wanted to handle the service." There was only one person Ron wanted and that was the senior pastor of the Methodist Church he had grown to love.

Ron was released from the hospital into the loving care of a hospice nurse named Susan – commonly referred to by Ann as an "Angel from God." Susan and Ron established a bond from the first day Susan stopped by the house. Maybe it was because Susan figured out that Ron and her husband, Robert, had graduated from the same high school. Or maybe the thread that tied them so closely together was the fact that Robert had passed away four years earlier of a similar brain tumor. Or could it be the fact that Susan had a daughter the exact same age as the Watson's daughter, Lisa? Whatever the reason, Ann knew Susan would soon become like family. "So not only had Susan walked where I was, but our husbands were at the same high school," recalls Ann. "Of all the people I could have gotten for a hospice nurse, she literally held my hand through three weeks of care and beyond. I remember her telling me to stop taking care of all the business and to just go sit with Ron. That was so hard to do. She encouraged me to take care of myself, and she encouraged the kids to crawl up in bed with their daddy where she would take pictures of them all. I would smile thinking how God did this for me. He loved me so and gave me this person in such a time of need. There's no way you can call that coincidental."

Although Ann prepared for what was imminent, she was unprepared to handle the affairs of Ron's law office. Thankfully attorney Jack Jones stepped in again and graciously volunteered to help sort the stacks of Ron's legal files, send letters to his clients, notify the courts and judges, and distribute all active cases. Ann was so grateful to Jack for his willingness to handle what she could not – another amazing provision from God. "This whole experience I feel for me has been cushioned by all these people God sent," Ann reflects. "When we'd get news, usually bad, my friend Cindy would call someone, and my friends at work would say it was like an army went in action in response to that call. I literally just pictured troops lining up." Ann was blessed with the peace of knowing that when she called upon friends, they would be there.

With all the amazing provisions God had blessed her with, Ann began to feel more relaxed about her financial future and her ability to care for her children without Ron. She recalls, "I got that stupid social security letter in the mail with proposed benefits. I never paid attention to it before, but I did now." With the monthly survivor benefit she would be entitled to, Ann realized they would not have to lose their house, and her children, despite losing their dad, would still have the security and comfort of their own home. Fearing judgment from others for worrying about her financial future, Ann never told Ron or anyone else about the social security letter. Ann says, "It was God reassuring me so I could focus on Ron—*I'm taking care of you Ann, the future is in My control; you be in the now and leave the rest to Me.* Family sat by Ron's side spending every possible minute with him until he joined his Lord and Savior in March 2008.

At thirty-two years old, nobody in the family contemplated nor prepared for Ron dying so young. In fact, just two weeks before his Christmas fall and original diagnosis, Ron had brought home all the information regarding his company's benefits of life and disability insurance, but Ann says they never found time to get to it. "I didn't miss that though," says Ann. "Provisions that came daily were so over the top, I really should be a servant to the church." Several months following the funeral, Ann came to a point where she felt not only provided for by her church family and community, but she also felt almost indulged because of the outpouring of support. "I needed to know that I could take care of the kids on my own," says Ann. "I was grateful, but I didn't want to take advantage. For instance, Troy's baseball coach, who only knew us for three months collected five hundred dollars and set up a sports account so Troy could continue to play baseball – that was his life." Troy's hockey coach participated in an Iron Man competition and donated his entire proceeds to us. And, a local law office chose Ann to be their first recipient of a special widow's fund. Those unexpected funds paid for Ron's funeral, some much-needed home repairs, and helped to establish a savings account. With so much community support, Ann says she felt a heavy sense of responsibility for what's been done.

That sense of responsibility was a challenge for Ann as gifts kept being abundantly provided to them. She was concerned her children might associate their father's death with the receipt of presents and money. One family gave the Watsons a Wii Game System that Ann saved to open on Ron's birthday. She used the occasion to explain to her kids about the humble family from their church that provided a way for them to have fun family time by purchasing a Wii. It was a gift to them on Ron's birthday. "We've done a lot of things to try and make Ron a constant memory in our house," says Ann. "I reassure my kids and confirm that it's okay to miss daddy. I tell them it's very sad but remind them how many great years they had with a man who absolutely adored them, who lived life, loved God, loved his family, and who was so proud of us that he told everyone whether they wanted to hear it or not. I tell them there are a huge percentage of people in the world who don't have any of that, so yes we can have our time to be sad but we're not going to stay feeling sorry for ourselves. We had daddy for a long period of time who was happy and healthy."

When asked how she handled getting through her first holidays Ann replied, "Father's Day stinks. Father's Day will probably never be okay. The first year's worth of holidays was more about me—my sadness. It was still very fresh. The second year I was more angry and hurt for my kids, because I could call my dad and wish him a Happy Father's Day, but my children didn't have their dad. There was not a lot I could do to ease that hurt. And now my children only have their grandpa, my dad, to call on Father's Day, because we also lost Ron's dad a year after Ron died."

As a new single mother of two, Ann contemplated changing her employment for the family's best interests. Her kids needed her home as much as possible, but she also had to provide financially for all their needs. However, God's plan was for Ann to remain where she was, surrounded by counselors who helped the children deal with their father's death, who advised Ann regarding the new discovery of her daughter's dyslexia, and who provided emotional support for Ann as a new widow. Ann recalls, "It was just another provision for me being at that place."

Thinking back Ann ponders, "What if the chair incident never happened and he was killed in a car accident? Would Ron be in Heaven? Out of all of this came Ron's salvation and probably my children's salvation. As much as I'd like to think I would have gotten on track at some point, I don't really know if I would have or not. We all were redirected in the way we needed to go because of what happened. His eternal life was changed because of the brain tumor." Ann recalls how Ron later laughed about falling off the chair saying he was just hard headed and how it took a bump on the head for him to figure it out. Comforted by the assurance Ron is in Heaven with Jesus and she will see him again one day, Ann looks ahead to God's new purpose for her life.

"I feel like I've worked through my grief in the sense that it's not a raw, open wound," says Ann. "Events are still somewhat painful and Ron was my soul mate, but I'm young and I feel there's still a love like that to come into my life." Ann is impatient for that process to start, but understands it must happen in God's timing and not hers. She describes her readiness with a wonderful visual picture, "You know when a child gets hurt how they run to their parents, climb up in their lap for comfort, and receive an embrace from their parent until they stop crying? Then, they eventually get down and go back to playing. That's how I felt. I feel in my time of grief I was sitting on God's lap, He was holding me and comforting me. As I started to feel better I sat up, looked around, and was ready to get down and go back to playing."

When asked how her relationship with God has changed through her painful experience, Ann simply states, "I've been in His lap." There she found everything she needed. Ann realized that she can't live daily sitting in His lap – she has to get down and go play. God is rebuilding a new relationship with Ann and although she admits her head knows that relationship must come first, her heart still longs for God to bring another amazing man into her life. While she waits, Ann says her heart knows God has her best interests at hand, and what He sees fit will be exactly what she needs. After all, it's her favorite word—providence.

Hope
Rev. Haas

Hope is the thing with feathers
That perches in the soul,
And sings the tune without the words,
And never stops at all,

And sweetest in the gale is heard;
And sore must be the storm
That could abash the little bird
That kept so many warm.

I've heard it in the chilliest land
And on the strangest sea;
Yet, never, in extremity,
It asked a crumb of me
—Emily Dickinson, "Poem 254," ca. 1861

This beautiful poem by Emily Dickenson compares the quality of hope with the characteristics of a bird. Hope flies, perches, sings and keeps the hopeless warm with its presence. Hope exists, and doesn't ask for anything in return; hope simply is.

Dickenson's poem alludes to the theological truth that hope is a gift of God. It is a gift that comes in the midst of the storm of our circumstances, a gift that appears in the coldest of situations, when we find ourselves unexpectedly thrust into a strange and unfamiliar place such as death. Hope cannot be abashed by even the deepest sorrow, and God imparts it to the griever to help them find warmth and solace in their loneliness. Hope floats.

So why is it then, that in the wake of a loved one's death, we feel so hopeless?

In the shock of the finality of death, we struggle with any concept of "tomorrow." Often our lives get stuck in that singular moment of change, when news of our loved one's death switches off life-as-we-knew-it and turns on life-as-we-can't-imagine-it. Hope abandons us like a runaway groom at an altar. All sense of a future is unfathomable to us; we can't imagine tomorrow, next week, or next month, much less a future without our loved one. And when our vision of time beyond today shuts down, hope shuts off. Some people even experience a reluctance to return to a place of looking forward, as though remaining in the permanent yesterday of life-before-death somehow honors the decedent or makes the love that they shared more real.

Let's take a look at a Biblical story of hope and see what we can learn.

In the second chapter of Acts, we see what happened to the disciples after Jesus' death. Jesus had appeared to many and offered convincing proofs that he was alive. For forty days he was with them, teaching them again about the kingdom of God and eating with them. He told them not to leave Jerusalem, for they are about to receive a great gift, a baptism of the Holy Spirit, which He had promised. They wondered if he was going to begin his reign then and finally restore the kingdom to Israel. He responds that it is not for them to know the time, but that they are called to be witnesses in Jerusalem, in Judea and Samaria, and to the ends of the earth. Immediately, He was taken up to heaven and left earth forever.

They returned to the Upper Room and devoted themselves to prayer. Matthias replaced Judas, and on the day of Pentecost, a violent wind came from heaven and tongues of fire came upon each one of them. They were filled with the Holy Spirit and began to speak and understand each other's tongues. Onlookers accused them of being drunk.

Peter stood to address the crowd and explained to them that the people weren't drunk, but rather filled with God's spirit, as prophesized by the prophet Joel. And then he told them of Jesus of Nazareth, a man known to them for his signs, wonders and miracles, who had been put to death by being nailed to a cross but had been raised from the dead by God. He concluded by quoting from King David:

> *"I saw the Lord always before me. Because he is at my right hand, I will not be shaken. Therefore my heart is glad and my tongue rejoices; my body also will rest in hope, because you will not abandon me to the realm of the dead, you will not let your holy one see decay. You have made known to me the paths of life; you will fill me with joy in your presence." (Acts 2:25-28, NIV 1984)*

This quote is stunning, coming at a time when the disciples must have been wavering in their faith. As Jesus ascended, they were left alone for the second and final time. He was gone from their midst again, seemingly not to return any time soon, if ever, in their lifetime. Leaderless and friendless, they gather together to pray and wait and BAM, they receive an outpouring of HIM.

In a significant way, Jesus' departure was marked by a part of Him being poured out into each of them. He gave them His power, His authority, His ability, and most importantly His presence—His living, vital, redeeming presence. They were empowered to preach

the Good News, teach, heal, and perform miracles. The flames, or
"tongues of fire" alighting on each head were an outward and visible
sign of the indwelling of Christ as he entered into them with an
inward, invisible grace.

Take a look again at verse 28:

> *"You have made known to me the paths of life; you will fill me
> with joy in your presence."*

The key to understanding the enormous hope in this passage is found
in this verse. When Peter says "you will fill me with joy IN your
presence," we automatically understand that to mean that when we
are with Jesus, it makes us happy. But another scripture sheds some
light on the characteristics of being IN Christ, where Paul makes the
strong connection between HOPE and being IN Christ:

> *"But you must stay deeply rooted and firm in your faith. You must
> not give up the hope you received when you heard the good news.
> It was preached to everyone on earth, and I myself have become
> a servant of this message. I am glad that I can suffer for you. I
> am pleased also that in my own body I can continue the suffering
> of Christ for his body, the church. God's plan was to make me
> a servant of his church and to send me to preach his complete
> message to you. For ages and ages this message was kept secret
> from everyone, but now it has been explained to God's people.
> God did this because he wanted you Gentiles to understand his
> wonderful and glorious mystery. And the mystery is that Christ
> lives IN you, and he is your hope of sharing in God's glory."*
> (Colossians 1:23-27, Contemporary English Version)

Paul actually had a lot to say on the subject of being IN Christ.
He speaks of being IN Christ, being "in UNION with Christ" and
"Christ IN you" approximately 172 times in one form or another in

his letters, according to Maxie Dunham. (Dunham, <u>Abiding in Christ</u> (Nashville: Upper Room Books, 2010) 66.) This isn't abiding with Christ or near Christ, but truly IN Christ. For Paul, the discovery of what happens when we abide in Christ is pivotal to our being able to have hope:

> *"Therefore if any person is [ingrafted] in Christ (the Messiah) he is a new creation (a new creature altogether); the old [previous moral and spiritual condition] has passed away. Behold, the fresh and new has come!" (2 Corinthians 5:17, Amplified Bible)*

Notice that in the Amplified Bible, the words "in-grafted in Christ" are used. This leads us to the passage in John that speaks directly to the idea of abiding in Christ as our source of hope:

The Vine and the Branches

> *"I am the true vine, and my Father is the gardener. He cuts off every branch in me that bears no fruit, while every branch that does bear fruit he prunes so that it will be even more fruitful. You are already clean because of the word I have spoken to you. Remain in me, as I also remain in you. No branch can bear fruit by itself; it must remain in the vine. Neither can you bear fruit unless you remain in me. "I am the vine; you are the branches. If you remain in me and I in you, you will bear much fruit; apart from me you can do nothing." (John 15:1-5, New International Version)*

So here is what we've learned:

1. In the midst of their loss of their beloved Jesus, the disciples were left with a piece of Him when He departed the earth.

2. That piece, the Holy Spirit, allowed Christ to dwell in them, and them in Him.

3. The mystery of faith revealed in Jesus' death is "Christ lives IN you, and he is your hope of sharing in glory."

4. We are made new by in-grafting ourselves to Christ.

5. Christ invites us to remain in Him, and He will remain in us. Only then will our lives bear fruit.

This is such good news for us who mourn. We have the assurance that even in these days of our loss, we can expect to be filled with Christ. When we allow His indwelling, we can have hope of a future. By living in Christ, the old life, yes, even the life we shared with our beloved departed, can be made new, and with an abiding of Christ in our new lives, we can bear fruit. All is not lost. All is not hopeless.

Now, let us consider a second type of indwelling that occurs—the indwelling that you have experienced with the person you loved who has died. Think about the things they said, the experiences you shared, the places you explored together, the tragedies and joys that were part of who you were together. Like the experience the disciples had at Pentecost, your memories allow you to receive a piece of your loved one that keeps that person alive in you, as you abide in them. As grief moves you along your relentless river of sorrow, you will find the void that the death has created will slowly, but surely, be replaced by the indwelling of a piece of them that remains IN you as the memories move in to fill the emptiness. You and your made-new life, filled with indwelling of your loved one, will bear the fruit of complete healing when you choose to abide in Christ and allow Christ to abide IN you.

Moving deeper into an abiding in Christ requires a few things of the believer.

First, we must immerse ourselves in the Scriptures. There is no substitute for this; daily, intentional Bible study is the first step to moving deeper into a life in Christ. Group Bible study should amplify personal reading, as God frequently will use other students to illuminate His Word to the individual. And the group interaction will be a place of community that bolsters you and helps you feel less lonely. Christ abides in those who study His word, and those who abide in Christ have hope.

The next step is to go further in your daily prayer life. Often in times of great sadness, we find that words simply fail us, and prayer becomes a struggle. The Scriptures attest to this:

> *"In the same way, the Spirit helps us in our weakness. We do not know what we ought to pray for, but the Spirit himself intercedes for us through wordless groans". (Romans 8:26, NIV 1984)*

When this happens, it is a good time to find a book of other people's prayers and read and pray through them. Denominational resources such as hymnals, books of worship, Psalters and prayer books might be available at your church. On-line prayer resources can be particularly helpful and easily accessible. Look for a Bible study on the subject of prayer, or seek out someone to serve as a prayer partner for you. Christ abides in those who pray, and those who abide in Christ have hope.

Practice other spiritual disciplines such as meditation, fasting, tithing, solitude, silence, worship, celebration, fellowship, and especially service. The phrase spiritual disciplines refer to practices that we choose to engage in so that we might receive God's grace, opening ourselves intentionally and deliberately to God's transformation.

In meditation, we quiet our sobbing long enough to hear God's whispered words of comfort.

In fasting, we remind our bodies of our soul's need for spiritual sustenance.

In tithing, we acknowledge that everything we have comes from God and a first fruit is due back to the One Who Gives.

In solitude, we shut out competing voices to focus on the One voice who brings peace to our hearts.

In silence, we stop the recurring recording that keeps playing in our heads of all the "should have/would have/wished we had/why didn't we" accusations, and rest from their relentless assault.

In worship, we focus our minds on God and not ourselves.

In celebration, we acknowledge that there is indeed a world outside of our mourning, and some of it contains joy.

In fellowship, we remind ourselves that we are not alone.

Christ abides in those who faithfully practice spiritual disciplines, and those who abide in Christ have hope.

All of these disciplines are important when seeking to abide in Christ and allowing Christ to abide in you, but of particular helpfulness to the mourner is the discipline of service. Serving Christ, whether by taking an occasional turn in the church nursery, teaching Sunday School, serving food at a local shelter or traveling overseas on a mission trip, is a sure way to get our eyes focused away from our hurt and onto a needy and hurting world. When we shift our attention thus, we see Christ, for surely He is in His world waiting to see His children served. There can be no greater reward for our work than to see a hungry child smile when handed a piece of bread, or an impoverished community rejoice at the building of a clinic. In these acts of service we become the hands and feet of Christ, but mourners also discover that we become the healed heart of Christ as well. And it is important to remember to serve in places where we have a spiritual gift, or God-given talent for that particular endeavor. Christ abides in those who serve, and those who abide in Christ have hope.

Let's go back now and take a second look at the passage from Acts 2:25-28 in a different translation:

> *"I saw God before me for all time. Nothing can shake me; he's right by my side. I'm glad from the inside out, ecstatic; I've pitched my tent in the land of hope. I know you'll never dump me in Hades; I'll never even smell the stench of death. You've got my feet on the life-path, with your face shining sun-joy all around."* (*Acts 2:25-28, The Message*)

As mentioned before, this passage comes after Jesus left the earth and the disciples were left behind. Peter is addressing the Jews about our Lord, and cleverly uses these words of King David to help make the connection.

Peter was quoting from Psalm 16, which was written by David at a time when King Saul was trying to kill him. David had fled to the mountain of Moan (how appropriate; have you been there recently?) and was in great fear for his life. Saul's army had encircled David, and death was inevitable. But then God provided a diversion, and David's life was spared. The early Hebrews learned to pray this Psalm whenever death was imminent.

What mourners can learn from this Psalm is that God is the One who sets our feet on the "life-path," as it says in the Message version, and that God never allows believers to even smell the stench of (eternal) death. We are called to pitch a tent in the land of hope in the face of death! We are called to see God's face, shining sun-joy in the face of death! We are invited to feel the Psalmist's ecstasy, for our loved one has also escaped (eternal) death. God is before us, for all time. Nothing can shake us; He is right by our side. Those who look death in the face and see God's face abide in Christ, and those who allow Christ to abide in them have HOPE. Your feet are on a life-path, not a death path. The message is clear: go forth and live.

This is how we can face tomorrow. This is how we can begin to live again, engaging in life around us, making plans and moving forward. This is why Jesus died on the cross for us, so that all who believe might have eternal life. And as to earthly life, Jesus was clear:

> "*The thief comes only in order to steal and kill and destroy. I came that they may have and enjoy life, and have it in abundance (to the full, till it overflows).*" (John 10:10, Amplified Bible)

This is why mourning only lasts for a season. Mourning is an important place of transition, adjustment, sadness and change, but only for a season. Abundant life is what Jesus promised, and He gives it so that we may enjoy life. Mourning is natural, automatic, and unavoidable, but only for a season. Abundant life is life that is lived to the full. Mourning is necessary, but only for a season. Abundant life is a life that overflows. As we read in Ecclesiastes:

> "*TO EVERYTHING there is a season, and a time for every matter or purpose under heaven: A time to be born and a time to die, a time to plant and a time to pluck up what is planted, A time to kill and a time to heal, a time to break down and a time to build up, A time to weep and a time to laugh, A TIME TO MOURN....AND A TIME TO DANCE.*" (Ecc. 3:1-4, Amplified Bible)

When your season of mourning is accomplished, don't forget to dance. While your season of mourning is in session, look forward to, and anticipate the dance. When your season of mourning threatens to overtake your life, proclaim the dance yet to come, and wait for its arrival....FOR YOU WILL DANCE. In the book of Jeremiah, we find these words that should be engraved upon every mourner's heart:

> *"I say this because I know what I am planning for you,"* says the Lord. *"I have good plans for you, not plans to hurt you. I will give you hope and a good future."* (Jeremiah 29:11, New Century Version)

And finally, one last thing before we go.

This book was written for believers, but it is our fervent prayer that perhaps some who will read it are not yet believers. If that is you, please listen. We believe that God is calling you to make that commitment to Him, right now, where you are. It is no accident that you found this book and have heard Him speaking to you through its pages. In the realm of God, there are no coincidences, only a prevenient grace that goes before us, wooing us and beckoning us to God's side where we will find hope, healing and life. These things aren't reserved just for a few, but are available to everyone. The invitation is openly given and free to all; "Come all of you, and abide in Me."

What God is asking of you in this moment is simply to do this. Bow your head and open your heart and let Him in. Invite Him into your life, with all of its sadness, mistakes, joys, complications, sins and triumphs. Ask Him to search you and to know you, and to take away your sins by the power of the cross. Acknowledge that He is God, and you are not. Tell him that you want to be saved, and that you believe that the only Savior is His son, Jesus Christ. And then invite Him to abide in you, and you in Him. Promise to follow Him all the days of your life.

And now it is done, and you are a Christ-follower! The angels rejoice in your decision, and know this for certain, you will never be alone again, you will never be without the comfort and guidance of your Heavenly Father, and you have joined a community of believers who stand with you in all things. Best of all, those who abide in Christ have HOPE. Halleluiah!

For believers, the invitation is to re-dedicate your life to Christ by praying the same prayer and inviting God's Spirit to come into you and lift you up. Open up your heart and renew your life of discipleship. Ask for cleansing and healing, and feel God filling you up with life-abundant. Thank Him for his faithfulness and re-dedicate your own faithfulness to Him. And be blessed, for you are now blessed to be a blessing to others. Halleluiah!

And at the end, there is just this: go now, and dance.

Amen.

> *Because He lives, I can face tomorrow,*
> *Because He lives, all fear is gone;*
> *Because I know He holds the future,*
> *And life is worth the living, just because He lives! (Bill Gaither,*
> *Because He Lives)*

About the Authors

Rev. Betsy Haas is an ordained United Methodist minister who holds an undergraduate degree in journalism from Penn State University. She attended seminary at the Candler School of Theology at Emory University in Atlanta, GA. She has over twenty years of combined ministry and professional writing experience. She has served the Peachtree City United Methodist Church in Peachtree City, Georgia, and is currently appointed to the Kitty Hawk United Methodist Church in Kitty Hawk, North Carolina. During the writing of this book, Rev. Haas lost her father very suddenly to a brain aneurysm and her beloved mother-in-law to Colon Cancer.

Lisa Mahaffey is a trained facilitator of a nationally renowned grief support program, where she has helped hundreds of grievers through their journey. She has also worked with children in grief through her local public school system. Her passion for helping those in grief comes from her own personal struggle after the loss of her husband at the age of twenty-six, and as caregiver for her father who died of cancer. Lisa is remarried, living in Atlanta, GA and has three sons.

CPSIA information can be obtained at www.ICGtesting.com
Printed in the USA
LVOW042021250113

317309LV00001B/2/P